ARCHITECTURAL DESIGN

EDITORIAL OFFICES:
42 LEINSTER GARDENS, LONDON W2 3AN
TEL: + 44 171 262 5097 FAX: + 44 171 262 5093

EDITOR: Maggie Toy
PRODUCTION EDITOR: Ramona Khambatta
ART EDITOR: Alex Young

CONSULTANTS: Catherine Cooke, Terry Farrell, Kenneth Frampton, Charles Jencks, Heinrich Klotz, Leon Krier, Robert Maxwell, Demetri Porphyrios, Kenneth Powell, Colin Rowe, Derek Walker

SUBSCRIPTION OFFICES:

UK: JOHN WILEY & SONS LTD
JOURNALS ADMINISTRATION DEPARTMENT
1 OAKLANDS WAY, BOGNOR REGIS
WEST SUSSEX, PO22 9SA, UK
TEL: 01243 843272 FAX: 01243 843232
E-mail: cs-journals@wiley.co.uk

USA AND CANADA:
JOHN WILEY & SONS, INC
JOURNALS ADMINISTRATION DEPARTMENT
605 THIRD AVENUE
NEW YORK, NY 10158 ·
TEL: + 1 212 850 6645 FAX: + 1 212 850 6021
CABLE JONWILE TELEX: 12-7063
E-mail: subinfo@wiley.com

ALL OTHER COUNTRIES:
WILEY-VCH GmbH
POSTFACH 101161
69451 WEINHEIM
FEDERAL REPUBLIC OF GERMANY
TEL: + 49 6201 606 148 FAX: + 49 6201 606 184

ANNUAL SUBSCRIPTION RATES 1997: UK £90.00, student rate: £65.00; Outside UK US$145.00, student rate: $105.00. Prices are for six issues and include postage and handling charges. Periodicals postage paid at Jamaica, NY 11431. Air freight and mailing in the USA by Publications Expediting Services Inc, 200 Meacham Ave, Elmont, NY 11003.

SINGLE ISSUES: UK £18.99; Outside UK $29.95. Order two or more titles and postage is free. For orders of one title please add £2.00/$5.00. To receive order by air please add £5.50/$10.00.

Printed in Italy. All prices are subject to change without notice. [ISSN: 0003-8504]

CONTENTS

Renzo Piano, New Metropolis, Amsterdam

ARCHITECTURAL DESIGN PROFILE No 130

CONTEMPORARY MUSEUMS

Adrian Wills, 'City Inhabitation Project'

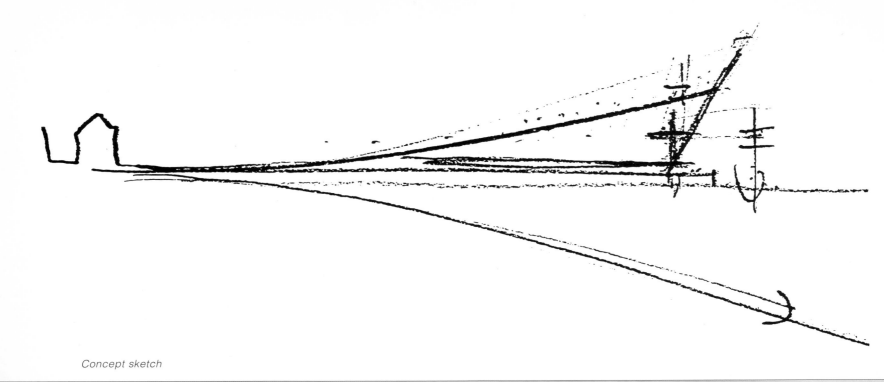

Concept sketch

RENZO PIANO BUILDING WORKSHOP

NEW METROPOLIS
Amsterdam, The Netherlands

Clad in oxidized copper and floating above a glass plinth, the new National Science and Technology Center's monumental form, rising up from the city's docklands, has a dramatic impact on the historic fabric of Amsterdam. Unsurprisingly, given its expressionist aesthetic, the building has been compared with numerous nautical forms, particularly with the prow of a 'great green supertanker', but this type of association, with its ugly mechanical overtones, does not do justice to the sensitivity of this urban intervention. In fact, the powerful aesthetic provides an excellent alternative to the retrogressive warehouse conversions that have proliferated during the recent regeneration of the waterfront.

The New Metropolis, as it is colloquially known, is located in the heart of Amsterdam, near to the social focus of the main station, on a man-made promontory above the entrance to the major road tunnel that passes under the Oosterdok. The form of the building, a truncated wedge gaining height as it travels away from the shore, is a direct response to the difficult nature of the site, rather than an attempt to produce a strong visual identity. However, the relationship between the city and the museum, is far more complex than the purity of the geometry would imply, and one which Renzo Piano has defined in the following terms:

> The building does not pretend to belong to the city, but wholly belongs to the docks. It does not lean, but 'floats' over the tunnel's entrance . . . the building establishes a gradual transition from the scale of the historic centre of Amsterdam to the openness of the harbour.

The site is accessed by a stepped walkway that rises up to meet the museum, creating an interesting juxtaposition to the two roads which disappear into the earth. The ramp and the roof define a single trajectory pulling away from the dense urban fabric.

As well as accessing the interior, the roof provides a terrace overlooking the city, exposing visitors to an aerial panorama of the city; particularly useful as it is almost impossible for the public to gain any vantage above street level in the city. Renzo Piano clarified the situation when he stated that:

> Amsterdam is known for being a flat city. It is one of the few in Europe where there are very few elevated public buildings, squares, terraces and bastions. Our roof terrace is probably the only public place in Amsterdam with a view over the historic city.

The rooftop piazza is also used as an open-air art gallery. There are currently a number of pieces by the Japanese sculptor Shingu and installations which exploit the kinetic energy of the environment, particularly the wind, sun and water. A second entrance is provided for water taxis, providing access through the glass envelope of the plinth into the main hall.

Constructing the centre above the tunnel also created a variety of structural problems that were tackled by the engineers Ove Arup and Partners. The main problem – the location of the building above a void – was resolved by supporting the lightweight steel frame on a heavily reinforced concrete slab which transfers the weight of the building onto the submerged piling located either side of the tunnel.

Internally, apart from the ground floor with its continuous glazing and the rooftop restaurant overlooking the city, the museum is orientated around a central lightwell that provides diffused light and spacial dynamics to the exhibition spaces. This works very well with the monolithic nature of exterior, and, in keeping with the smooth aesthetic, the few windows that actually puncture the envelope are latticed and flush, allowing the cladding to continue uninterrupted over them. The blank expanse of the external walls is also reflected in the austerity of the interior, described by Piano as 'frugal and simple', allowing visitors to focus on the exhibits rather than visual gymnastics. The museum includes permanent and temporary interactive exhibitions illustrating various aspects of communication, energy, humanity, phenomena and technology.

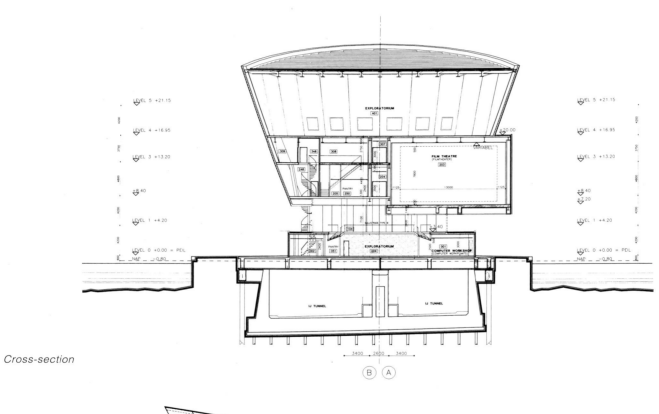

Cross-section

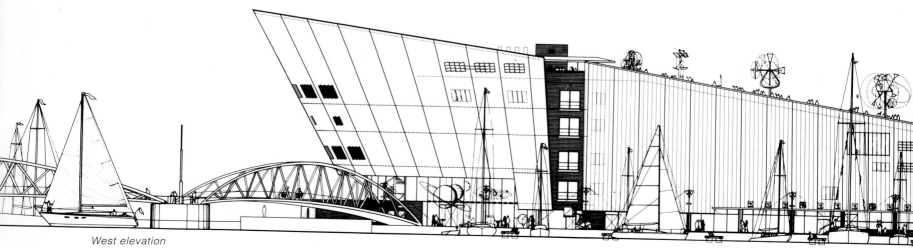

West elevation

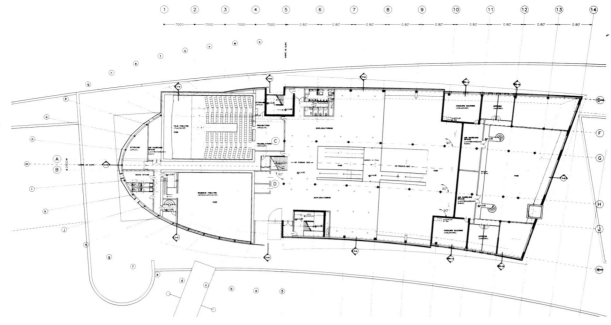

Third floor plan

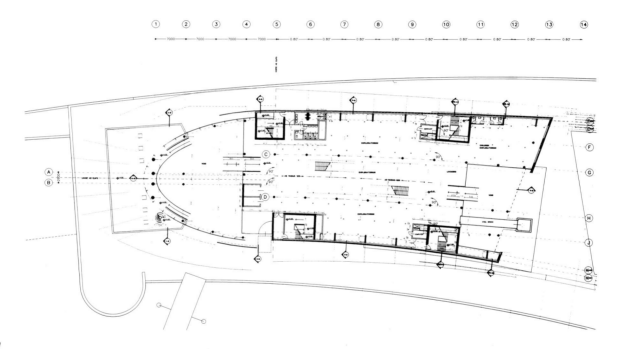

First floor plan

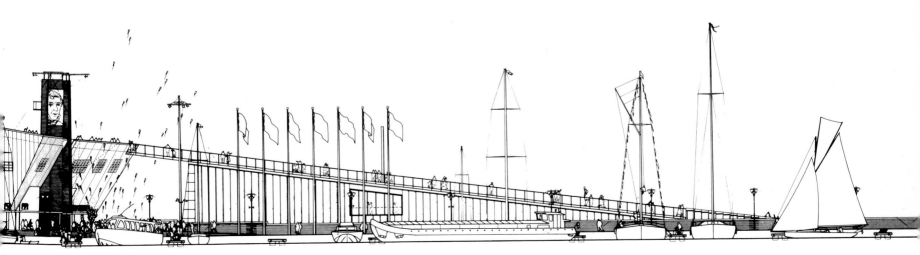

V

City of the Dead, Cairo

Settlement 3 Katameya

Unfinished Bridge, Abassaya, Cairo

Road out of Nasr City (towards New Cairo), informal settlements

Clubhouse, Katameya

Mubarak City, New Cairo

CULTURE CLASH
THE DEVELOPMENT OF NEW CAIRO
Eleanor Curtis

New Cairo in context

The desert development of New Cairo, City 2000 or City of the Future, may soon be the Beverly Hills of the Middle East, whose inhabitants will enjoy a life of luxury and golf courses, wide avenues and grand villas. A city for the bold and beautiful.

Standing high above the vibrant metropolis of Cairo proper, a city of over 17 million inhabitants living in and around its numerous historic centres, New Cairo is to offer a new way of life, a new model of urban design, all in keeping with world-wide globalisation and open market economy.

Listed by the World Heritage, Cairo's architectural treasures include some 620 historic monuments dating back to the original 7th-century city of Fustat. Though the Great Pyramids of Giza have stood the test of tyrants, earthquakes and colonisation over 4,000 years, the Sphinx now stares at the bright neon of Pizza Hut and Kentucky Fried Chicken. These global signs of the times may also be seen reflected in Cairo's new urban policies.

The new residential city

New Cairo is a two-year-old urban development scheme that links with the main city, extending it by 60% of its original size east into the desert on the Suez Road. Cairo proper currently spans some 11km by 14 km giving a total area of nearly 180km² on desert land. New Cairo represents the desired urban life for the top slice of Caireans, or so its planners project.

Since the late 70s Egypt's urban planners have commenced an 'ambitious programme to build a series of new communities to redistribute population and economic activities, protect agricultural land, create job opportunities and upgrade the quality of the living environment' as officially stated by the Ministry of Housing, Utilities and Urban Communities. This has resulted in the public construction of industrial-based cities on the outskirts of Cairo, like 6th October and 10th Ramadan, in the hope of attracting a skilled work-force, and the selling off, to private investors and wealthy individuals, of a decent sized chunk of desert land.

Unlike the other new cities, New Cairo will be a residential city based around services rather than industry or agriculture, with an estimated 60/40 split between the two on available building land. It has an average altitude of 250m above sea-level, and looks down on landmarks like the Mohammed Ali Mosque of Cairo's old city in the distance. New Cairo is well connected with the existing suburbs of Maadi, Heliopolis and Nasr City via its direct linkage with the ring road.

The land has been split into a number of large sectors: President Mubarak's new Police Academy is located to the north-west and is currently operational; individual plots are concentrated around the soon-to-be-developed central service axis, which runs through the city centre; two golf courses are being located at either end of the western edge of the city boundaries; while the development of Katameya to the south, sits beneath the youth housing scheme Mubarak City.

The residential areas are to include two types of development: land parcels of 600m² for individuals and large tracts of land for private developers. The individual residencies are aimed at two types of client: the single family, consisting of a private villa with swimming pool and garden, and the younger generation, providing small apartments at subsidised rates. A proposed circular axis inside the city is considered as an artery between residential parts and other services: including commercial centres, green and open spaces, recreational activities, sporting clubs, cultural centres, theatres and cinemas, in addition to administrative, social and religious activities. Maximising green space is a priority, using recycled water from desalination plants to irrigate the land.

The urban designers talk of the extensive use of new technologies and communications in their designs, which utilise an intelligent road system, wide open avenues and self-contained units. The New Cairo resident will not have to venture out of the city for work, leisure or services, as it will offer a complete urban package – new schools, hospitals, offices, and shopping centres – completely eradicating the need to go to downtown Cairo.

The current transportation and communication systems that exist in congested Cairo proper will be replaced with a new model of city life, including an up-to-date infrastructure that will complement the busy, demanding, techno-lifestyle of its new executives and families. Currently, Caireans commute from one side of town to another for work and leisure, spending vast amounts of time inhaling the pollutants of the consistent traffic jams.

The official response to such an affluent development in the context of the city's existing urban problems is to 'absorb' the ever-expanding population of Cairo's 17 million inhabitants, and encourage a shift in population away from the city centre. It is hoped that shortly after the year 2000, with an estimated annual population increase of 2%, the number of inhabitants in the city centre will be reduced to 12-13 million, with the other 5-7 million distributed amongst these new cities. New Cairo alone is expected to absorb approximately 2.5 million inhabitants.

American dreams and new landmarks

New Cairo's relationship to Cairo's heritage seems minimal. Previous urban growth was centred around the mosque, as in Islamic Cairo, or around the industrial factory or commercial district, as in post-revolutionary Egypt. Today the master planners have chosen an American model of a service city, where the golf course will act as the new landmark.

Space Consultants, a firm specialising in architecture and urban design, based in downtown Cairo, with 250 employees and an impressive list of other large-scale urban designs for Egypt in their resume, are solely responsible for the urban plan of New Cairo, reporting directly to the Ministry of Housing and Redevelopment.

Led by Dr Medhat Dorrh, professor at Cairo University's Department of Architecture and Planning and Director of Space Consultants since his return to Cairo from the US in 1980, the rationale behind the American model of urban design is explained in terms of the recent shift in modern Cairean lifestyles, a result of President Mubarak's open-door economic policies. Dorrh himself has described the situation as follows:

> There have been many dramatic economic and social changes in Cairo over the last 15 years. The modern Egyptian is now exposed to so many different cultures that he cannot be forced to live in a traditional Arab way. We are now looking at one international or global language of urban expression and this is reflected in the way of living.

True to Dorrh's words, one need only take a look around, while immobilised in one of Cairo's traffic jams, to see the latest model BMWs, Mercedes and Jaguars with the driver behind the wheel making business calls on his mobile phone.

Regarding the effect of this globalisation on Cairo's architecture, Dorrh justifies the use of imported models due to the level of eradication of local design that has already occurred:

> There is no such thing as local architecture any more, the sheer speed of transport and telecommunications have changed the notion of what is local. Within a few hours of Cairo you can be in the heart of Europe dazzling the eye with a different set of architectural styles. The client reflects this exposure in his choice of new non-traditional models.

Entering into this global context of design and planning, Dorrh is pushing the advantages of the wider scale of urban design adopted in the US, combined with a calculated and efficient infrastructure. Having undergone his architectural and urban planning education at the University of Pennsylvania, Dorrh is all too familiar with the American urban strategies. The model chosen promotes a new concept of housing for the Middle East, where front gardens are set back from the road, with footpaths and fences between villas separating one neighbour from another. There will be no gaps left between residential areas to allow community improvisation – as exists in the streets of Cairo today where the *bowab* (caretaker) and other service employees resourcefully make use of any space, at street or roof level.

The villas themselves, some of which are commissioned out to individual architects and some designed by Space Consultants, must adhere to certain specified criteria: the character is defined as Spanish or Mediterranean style, typically with arched windows and gabled roofs, a maximum of 13m in height and of restricted colour. The villas designed by Space Consultants are offered on a ready-made basis, with varying degrees of luxury. Market prices start at 400,000 LE (£80,000) continuing up to 2 million LE (£400,000).

Authentic afterthoughts – an attempt to celebrate the past
One local architectural practice that is currently catering to the tastes of the new client is Gamal Bakry and Associates. Participants in the 1995 Venice Biennale, they have been commissioned to design six luxury villas and a private school for New Cairo in Katameya.

Bakry prides himself on his modern abstractions from traditional styles of Arab architecture, but expresses his disappointment at the unimaginative brief from his clients:

> There is little creativity to a Spanish style villa. My clients come with *House and Garden* under their arms to our meetings, and demand something from the glossy pages.

They have little understanding of style; they look at Western art and architecture and want to imitate it, without really understanding it. They want Italian facades without any idea of the context.

The husband and wife team aim to incorporate some inclination toward Arab architecture in their designs, with their use of the courtyard, small windows and pergolas. As they explain:

> Building in the desert environment demands solutions to climatic problems. Though the American model is seen as desirable it is also very expensive: the land must be extensively irrigated and extra shading must be designed to combat the large open spaces from the heat.

They too are recipients of the wave of change that is hitting Egyptian culture, so the pro-American attitudes come as no surprise, especially considering that their clients are all in some way associated with America, whether through formal education or business. Their personal vision of the future Cairo is likened to Los Angeles with its interlinking ring roads, wide avenues, shopping malls, downtown areas and efficient metro (plus some token ghettos that already exist).

In addition to the villas that Space Consultants are designing, they are also responsible for the central service axis, occasionally known as the Central Business District. This area is designed as one long spine, 8km in length, that runs through the centre of New Cairo, reminiscent of the Fatamid thoroughfare, Sherra Muizz Lidin Allah, that runs the length of the quarter. The designs of the buildings will mix various elements of the old Islamic with the new ideas of post-modernism, carving history into new stone. As the master planner Dorrh articulates:

> Any theoretical model must be able to cope with the projected needs of the future community. It is very difficult to start a city with old character. However, the centre of New Cairo will copy elements of old Cairo from its pedestrian spine, so as you walk through you will be reminded of old Cairo – using an old gate at one end of the spine and a new post-modern styled gate at the other end.

The spine is intended to be fully pedestrianised, but with convenient accessibility and parking facilities running along the length of the city centre.

Carpeting the desert green
The Katameya development, with over 1.6 million m² of land to play with to the south-west corner of New Cairo, boasts the most exclusive golf course in Egypt. Set in the dusty yellow desert sands, amid a backdrop of construction sites, Katameya Golf and Tennis Resort offers a stunning view of what New Cairo might one day have to offer: rolling green landscapes with artificial lakes and a Mediterranean style clubhouse, reminiscent of the grand colonial days, which emits an atmosphere of sheer luxury and affluence.

The manicured 27-hole golf course is carpeted with fresh Georgian turf, flown in from Atlanta in refrigerated crates. Created by French designer Yves Bureau, the turf is being carefully maintained and extended by a resident Floridian expert. Some of the luxury villas are woven into the course design, providing beautiful landscaped views for the residents and, in turn, a regular healthy income for course maintenance.

Developer of Katameya, and director of the Arab Sunley Construction Company, Khaled Abou Taleb echoes Dorrh's views on the current shift of cultural values in Egypt:

> The display of wealth today is a new trend of confidence – confidence with the government for the wealthy businessman

so that he feels comfortable to display his wealth in the purchase of a luxury villa. Ten years ago a project like this would have been termed 'aggressive', but today the new money is staying in the country and the people want to show it.

Enticing the young generation

In addition to the Katameya developments, are the already constructed apartment blocks of Mubarak City. This sector has been subsidised by the government to offer reasonably priced apartments to the newly-wed, middle-class, first time home buyer. In Cairo proper, young brides and grooms are unable to purchase their first home due to extortionate prices for relatively poor quality housing, and are subsequently forced to delay the wedding day or remain under their parents' roofs. The four- and five-storey apartment blocks are situated downhill from the Katameya Resort, decorated in an assortment of bright positive colours, and marketed as offering not just a home but a new healthy environment.

Peripheral wasteland or gold-mines?

New Cairo is an impressively fast development. Within the last two years, what was considered to be peripheral wasteland is now looked upon as a real estate gold-mine. The rapid sale of this large piece of desert is a little bewildering considering that the land was previously designated for resettling the ever-growing informal communities, after extensive research by Government planners five years ago. In fact, the official 'absorption of population' methodology does not appear to be apparent in New Cairo's extensive urban plans over the next 15 years.

Some of these resettlement plans were acted upon and resulted in three public housing developments, known as Settlements 1, 3 and 5, in the New Cairo area. To the embarrassment of the government, this drab housing that came free with the land package, is now sitting on prime development sites.

These tower blocks were erected in 1992 as emergency shelters for those displaced in the dramatic earthquake that hit the city in October that year. There could not be more of a contrast between the luxurious air-conditioned bars, with views of manicured lawns, and the cracked grubby tower block slums, with puddles of sewage in the streets, especially considering that they are within five minutes walk of each other. Fortunately for the planners and golfers, Settlement 3 is on a low contour and does not offend the players.

However, the potential eyesore that these settlements may cause potential residents has already put their future under threat. After scandalous rumours in the Egyptian press in June 1997,[1] stating that the Housing Minister was to order 129 buildings to be demolished, he has since backed off, informing the public that not all of them will be dismantled, and that those remaining will be given an emergency face-lift 'more in keeping' with the rest of New Cairo.

Facing Settlement 3 are some of the city's Christian dead, interned in a sprawling cemetery, with crosses jaggedly decorating the sky. For over five centuries, the availability of land in Cairo, for the living and the dead, has been minimal. In fact, since the 15th century the pressure on urban space forced people to take up permanent residence in some of the Mamluke cemeteries, resulting in the living necropolis known as The City of the Dead. The more recent cemeteries have been pushed to beyond the city's ring road, to cheap, but accessible areas. New Cairo's Christian ghosts were part of this move, but no more dead are to take up the now precious land. The new cemeteries are now located south of the city, on the road to Fayoum.

Thriving informal communities

Just south of New Cairo are some of the numerous informal settlements of Cairo, easily identified by the mounting rubbish heaps and discarded building materials. These improvised communities, with their makeshift factories and sweat-shops, make up a surprisingly large proportion of Cairo's economic sector: there are an estimated 80 informal settlements contained within the city's limits.[2]

With a lack of attention on the rural areas of developing countries world-wide and heavy concentration on new industry and services, Egyptian villages are being ignored and there continues to be a steady influx of populace to the city streets.

Dr Leila Iskander, urban environmentalist and Director of the NGO Community and Institutional Development, Cairo, is disappointed at the exclusive concentration on new developments by the city planners, rather than focusing on the urban problems that plague the city today:

> Where has the imagination gone in urban development plans? How can anyone leave places like Islamic Cairo to rot? The Islamic quarter is Cairo's jewel, these are the streets of Naguib Mahfouz's evocative stories. Presently both these areas are unsuitable environments in which to live or even have an office, but the urban problems therein are not without solutions. Traffic congestion, dirt, overcrowding, poor sanitary conditions, can all be solved with enough time and energy. It is not as if we are without resources.

She favours a reshuffling of urban priorities that will at least provide the very poor with the basic infrastructure for a healthy life, pointing out that the informal settlements still do not have access to running water or electricity, as they are not officially recognised by the government. Within the Gamaleya district, a formal community in the Islamic quarter which has a population density of 275,000 in under 4km², over 33% of all dwellings are still not connected with a fresh water supply. Referring to the general co-operation that exists between all classes of city dwellers, Iskander highlights the tolerated improvisation of spaces by the low class service employees in sometimes very affluent areas, claiming that such cross-overs do not necessarily reduce the posh residential building to a slum:

> The rich and the poor have always lived on top of each other in this city. The *bowab* (caretaker) or the *makwagee* (clothes ironer) might be living in the ground floor or roof of the same building as the director of the largest company in Egypt. This is how Caireans live and have always lived. Creating this isolated area for the elite seems to be at the expense of the cultural heritage of the city, missing out from the hubbub of the city that constitutes the very life-force, the backbone of the culture.

Practising architect Abdel Haleem Ibrahim Abdel Haleem, winner of the Aga Khan Award in 1992, specialises in community design and rehabilitation in the Islamic quarter of the city and knows the urban problems of the city intimately. Whilst not critically opposing the idea of grand and interesting villas extending the city boundaries, he points to the potentially distorted image they can give to Egypt's cultural perceptions:

> If the architecture and urban plan was to enhance the environment, then great! But these villas are antagonistic. It

slaps the poor majority in the face with an outrageous expression of exclusive wealth. Is this really necessary? We have always had wide divisions between rich and poor, but at least the previous architectural palaces of Cairo respected the common cultural heritage.

Agreeing with the dramatic affects that globalisation has had on world-wide culture, he does not see this as a reason for eradicating local architecture – one should not exclude the other.

Previous eras of grand architectural developments, Abdel Haleem comments, have always transcended their boundaries to benefit local culture. He cites the example of the colonisation of Cairo by the British in the late 19th century, that brought lush garden city villas and characterised the downtown area with elements of Paris. Though originally imitating European cities, these designs also played on the local architecture, creating an ornate, sometimes kitsch, Islamic style. The current imports of urban design, however, do not appear to distil any knowledge that is beneficial to the local community. As Abdel Haleem articulates, 'What are we learning from these new model cities? They do not even possess a *midan* (central square or piazza) to attract a local community and age before they have even begun!'

Cairo's layers of dust, debris and history
Since the late 50s, Cairo city has grown tall and wide, and today one may speak of many centres, ever-growing peripheries and layers of history collected in the city's dust. The city boundaries have become blurred since the spread of informal communities, and the traditional centres have lost their attraction due to a combination of neglect and the emergence of 'modern' sectors.

The area of Islamic Cairo that houses some of the region's finest monumental treasures, like the Ibn Tulun Mosque or the Khan el-Khalili bazaars, is burdened with an out-of-date infrastructure that simply cannot support its residents and traders. With its bustling, thriving community this quarter cannot simply be conserved, like some museum piece, in isolation to the needs of the resident community.

Downtown Cairo used to be the centre for commercial activity and the popular shopping area of the earlier part of the 20th century, but with the post-revolutionary development of areas like Mohandiseen and Dokki, with their tall office blocks and apartment buildings, activities have become dispersed. Suburbs were designed to ease the city's congestion but, they too, now suffer their own architectural congestion of tower blocks. Land prices have soared and building space is at a premium. The grand old villas of the late 19th century, rather than being revered for their architectural heritage, are seen as obstructing land from realising its full economic potential.

Within the modern areas of Cairo, building regulations have been largely ignored and have proliferated an ugly landscape of heights and characterless structures. The soon-to-be-reviewed housing law, introduced by Gamal Abdel Nasser in the 50s, froze all rents and has subsequently allowed most of the old buildings to fall down due to insufficient maintenance funds.

For most Caireans, a significant proportion of daily life is spent in a traffic jam, admiring the inside of a third-floor apartment block or one of the city's many building boards. The skies are littered with (sometimes unfinished) flyovers, shadowing the streets down below. Donkeys and Mercedez intermingle in the afternoon congestion, each competing at an average of 10km per hour.

With a population growth of 1.25 million per year, and 95% of them living on 3% of available land, Cairo is being pushed to its limits. The average wage of a public sector employee is between 300-500 LE (£60-100) per month, which accounts for 34% of the working population. The 1996 estimated per capita income was just over £400 per year (£33 per month) and, just 5% of the population are estimated to have incomes of 700,000 LE (£140,000) and over – just about enough to purchase one of the luxurious villas of New Cairo.[3]

A new identity for the Middle East?
On a more positive note, President Mubarak's open-door economic policies, clearly reflected in New Cairo's real estate architecture, are encouraging Egyptians to put their money back into the country's economy. One need only look at the booming construction industry along Egypt's Red Sea coasts, to see recent investment trends in model tourist resorts.

The doors to foreign investment have also been opened wider than ever before, allowing other Middle Eastern investors to have a share in the takings. New Cairo already has money coming from Kuwait, Jordan and Saudi Arabia, through joint ventures with other Caireans. Unlike Beirut, which is vertically arranged on a small land area and focusing on rebuilding its damaged infrastructure, New Cairo is a brand new horizontal city offering clean air and green spaces, offering a new way of life. The planners see New Cairo as the archetypal Middle Eastern city.

To allow Cairo to lead the Middle East with a strong identity, the city requires a strong centre. Unfortunately, it appears that this centre has been worn down by enormous population pressures on a poor infrastructure, rigid housing laws that have left frozen rents for over 40 years, and the impact of out-of-context global consumer culture, resulting in a heavily congested and polluted historic city. Even the formal developments of the peripheries need a centre to refer to, to depend on, around which to focus. So the important question is whether the New Cairo model offers anything to ease these urban problems? Most critics think not, viewing New Cairo as an isolated island of prosperity, in the middle of some of the most depressed and impoverished areas of Cairo, far removed from Egyptian life and culture. The American model of living is seen as completely inappropriate to a culture that is entrenched in many centuries of manners and customs – Egyptian habits die hard.

Notes
1   *Cairo Times*, Cairo, June 1997
2   Community and Institutional Development figures 1997
3   1996 census from *Practical Guide to Cairo*, AUC Press, Cairo, 1997

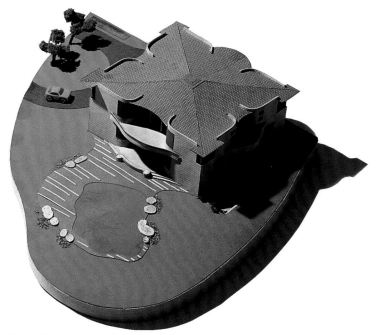

Gamal Bakry, model of private villa, New Cairo

Cairo Cityscape from Ring Road

Building boards, Möhandiseen, Cairo

Fatamid thoroughfare, Cairo

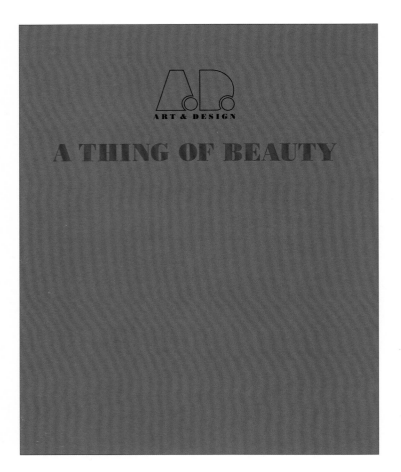

A THING OF BEAUTY IS . . .

Guest-edited by Michael Petry

ART & DESIGN PROFILE 54

Perhaps the worst thing that can be said of modern art is that it is beautiful. This dismisses the work as mere fluff: art that is candy; art that is not really art. This profile explores beauty as a cultural construct, looking both at its more positive historical associations and how it functions today in relation to artworks in the global media age. With contributions from over 40 different artists and writers, *A Thing of Beauty is . . .* will ask if anything can be allowed to be beautiful again, and, if so, what does it mean for art in what is perceived to be an ugly age, or is the myth of the ugly only the other side of the looking-glass?

Michael Petry, artist, writer and Co-Director of the Museum of Installation, London, also guest-edited the A&D profile *Abstract Eroticism*.

PB 0 471 97684 9, 305 x 250 mm, 96 pages. Illustrated throughout, mainly in colour. £19.99 $32.50 May 1997

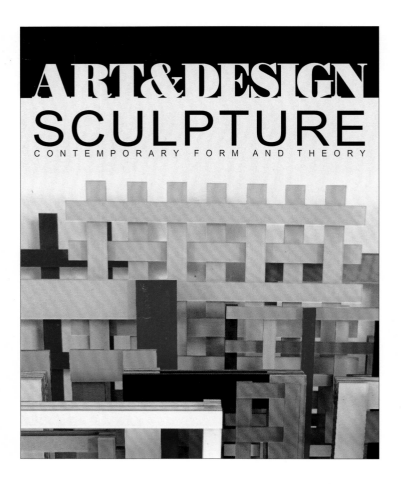

SCULPTURE: CONTEMPORARY FORM AND THEORY

Guest-edited by Andrew Benjamin

ART & DESIGN PROFILE 55

The renewal of interest in the art object has led to a rethinking of the nature of sculpture. This stimulating issue presents a highly-illustrated survey of European and American sculpture, from the 1970s to the present day, in the context of recent thought. Articles by leading theorists, critics and philosophers include: Saul Ostrow looking at post-minimal sculpture in the USA; Stan Allen on minimalism in architecture and sculpture; David Batchelor on colour in sculpture; Rebecca Comay on Rachel Whiteread's proposal for a Holocaust Memorial in Vienna; David Moos on Harald Klingelhöller; Charles Harrison on David Batchelor; Jean-Luc Nancy on Lucille Bertrand, and Jesse Reiser on Tony Cragg.

Andrew Benjamin is Professor of Philosophy at the University of Warwick and has been widely published. His most recent titles published by Academy Editions include *Object Painting* and *What is Abstraction?*

PB 0 471 976946, 305 x 250 mm, 96 pages, Illustrated throughout, mainly in colour. £19.99 $32.50 July 1997

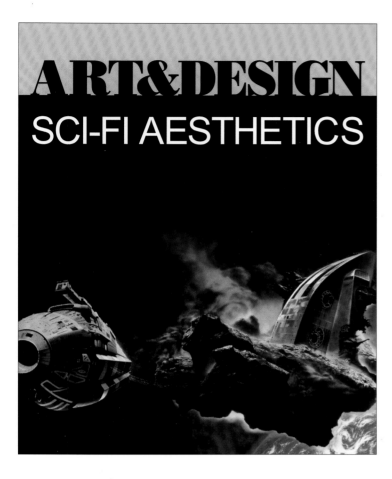

SCI-FI AESTHETICS

Guest-edited by Rachel Armstrong

ART & DESIGN PROFILE 56

Asserting that science fiction is the integration of art and science, this issue of *Art & Design* seeks to answer the question, 'What will it be like to be human in the future?' Examining the work of contemporary artists such as Orlan, Stelarc, the Chapmans, Mariko Mori, Peter Gabriel and Kathy Acker, it also includes a wide variety of writings with contributions from scientists, doctors and fiction writers. The focus is on the human body as a metaphor to reflect our hopes, fears and anxieties about our ability to survive and evolve in an increasingly information-overloaded and technological world.

Dr Rachel Armstrong is a multi-media and science fiction specialist based in London. She has written extensively on issues concerning art, science and technology.

PB 0 471 97855 8, 305 x 250 mm, 96 pages. Illustrated throughout, mainly in colour. £19.99 $32.50
September 1997

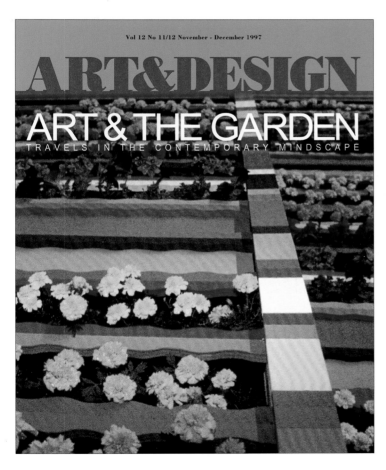

ART & THE GARDEN

Guest-edited by Anne de Charmant

ART & DESIGN PROFILE 57

Presenting the garden as a major contemporary art form, this issue of *Art & Design* examines some of the most exciting international developments in this field, exploring the special nature of the garden in our collective consciousness. There are a diverse range of contributions including: Yves Abrioux defining a contemporary 'gardenesque'; Stephen Bann on the links between land art and the garden landscape; John Stathatos on the continuing battle of Little Sparta and the garden of Ian Hamilton Finlay; Charles Jencks on his own garden in Scotland, and Günter Nitschke on contemporary Japanese gardens. Other features include: Ronald Jones' Caesar's Cosmic Garden; Rüdiger Schottle's Theatre Garden; Derek Jarman's garden at Dungeness; the Festival of Gardening at Chaumont sur Loire, and the designs of Gilles Clément, Newton Harrison and Helen Mayer Harrison and Meg Webster.

Anne de Charmant is a writer and curator based in London

PB 0 471 978 558, 305 x 250 mm, 96 pages. Illustrated throughout, mainly in colour. £19.99 $32.50
November 1997

Books

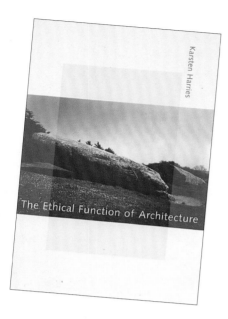

The Ethical Function of Architecture by Karsten Harries, MIT Press (Cambridge, MA), 1997, 403pp, 123 b/w ills, £29.95

This book uses German philosophy to act as a model, or lens, to elucidate the so-called 'contemporary condition'. What sets it apart from previous works is that the author attempts to go beyond the fashionable nihilistic critique of the present to suggest a positive way forward for architecture based on the reintroduction of an ethical dimension.

Harries' central thesis is presented as a gentle polemic which is explored through a collection of 24 essays, grouped into four thematic sections. The first set of essays attacks the aesthetic interpretation of architecture, the second considers problems of the language of architecture, the third looks at Heidegger's ideas on the relationship between building and dwelling, and the fourth explores the relationship between public and private architecture, promoting the necessity for architecture to carry collective expression.

The contents of the book demonstrate a thorough and impressively wide-ranging knowledge of architecture and architectural theory, gained partly through the author's long-standing relationship with the Yale University School of Architecture. The discussions are lucid and engaging, and made all the more persuasive by the application of the precise language of philosophy. Inevitably this can be dense and complex and is not for the faint-hearted. Although a prior knowledge of philosophy is not essential, the author's phenomenological perspective and frequent references to Heidegger, Hegel and Nietzsche, means that some familiarity with their writings is necessary for a full engagement with the text.

The design of the book is striking in its restraint; the simple typeface, the single column of text and the few carefully chosen black and white illustrations combine to convey the seriousness of this work.

Trespassing across academic boundaries is a dangerous occupation. However, in this case Harries has demonstrated a remarkably wide-ranging knowledge and understanding of architecture. The result is a valuable and thought provoking contribution to architectural theory, which deserves to exercise a formative influence on contemporary architectural practice.

Helena Webster

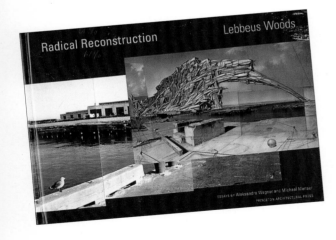

Radical Reconstruction by Lebbeus Woods, Princeton Architectural Press (New York), 1997, 168pp, ills throughout in colour & b/w, HB £30.00

If you are expecting this to be an objective review you will be sadly disappointed. This book is about subjectivity. Lebbeus Woods has an interest in the human subject and the human condition that far exceeds the normative meanderings of traditional architectural practice. Humanity, its liberation, its catastrophes (both natural and unnatural) and its freedom, is central to this work. It is a book against 'zero tolerance'. It is a book about the mitigation of pain, strife and political and aesthetic bondage. Even more remarkably, it believes that architecture is of value in this context.

Radical Reconstruction is an apt title. It takes us on a journey – some paths are implied, some are explicit – that questions and reformulates architecture's constituent parts. One by one meaning, function, representation, abstraction et al, are run through the mill and recast within the contexts of war and cataclysmic social and physical fracture.

The projects are set in Sarajevo, Havana and San Francisco, and they simultaneously mediate many boundaries. Like Woods' concept of 'free space', the book itself has much 'elbow room' for the reader. It leaves a huge amount unsaid. This I like. The fact that as a viewer/reader I can bring my own preoccupations to bear on the images: imagining other worlds and other technologies that may have been used to create such distinct yet fluctuating architecture. Like the architecture, the drawings are not exclusively pragmatic or poetic. There is 'oblique' space within the work which fosters personal readings. This is tolerance of another kind.

Woods tolerates, but is not ambivalent about, cruelty towards people or blind human perseverance and survival. He attempts to ease all these dilemmas, but at the same time finds a creative struggle. As Captain Beefheart has said, 'the way I keep in touch with the world is very gingerly because it touches too hard.' Woods' work is insurance against this hard touch and also uses some of the hardest touches the world has to give creatively. Woods refuses to accept 'normal' architecture in all its manifestations. 'Normal' architecture is nothing if not a conspiracy of capitalist vested interests, social manipulation and aesthetic fascism.

This book is a critique against the rhetoric of reductivism and minimalism. This is 'full on' maximist architecture. It is an acknowledgement that the practice of architecture exists within a beautiful complexity.

Neil Spiller

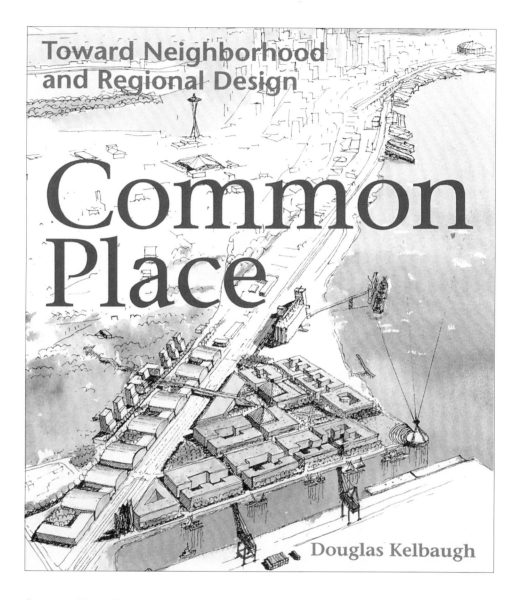

Common Place: Toward Neighborhood and Regional Design *by Douglas Kelbaugh, University of Washington Press (Seattle and London), 1997, 334pp, 100ills b/w, PB $35.00*

Common Place summarises eight design workshops located around the city of Seattle, which 'develop convivial and sustainable places in the face of fast-paced growth'. These projects respond to the problems of a changing future of high-density urban life and present essentially reactive responses to research; while the conceptual work reveals too few of the sort of exciting opportunities that are changing social, industrial and healthcare aspects of life and planning in western cities today. If this work was to become part of an ongoing exhibition of findings/updated projects, it could be used to forecast or instigate the imminent changes that worry the planners of Seattle, but in book form the graphics are disparate and the bar charts and diagrams seem to clash with the graphics of improvised brainstorming. The schemes face-up to infrastructure problems in concerned isolation; whereas the workloads, care, leisure pursuits and general demographics of the people moving into this town might have offered more generous/ flexible approaches, that would have involved more than simply the fabric of the town.

Common Place has plenty of background research into population, housing stock and transport statistics; in one section it also looks at the households of Seattle. More people will probably live alone, share flats and become increasingly dependent on more services as the population gets older – but the book's thorough analysis of transport systems neglects to include the delivery of services which many governments and industries now offer. As industry and workforces become more flexible and distant, less distinction is being made between buildings and the envelope of care/maintenance services and products that surround them. It's a shame that this panoramic research didn't recognise some of these opportunities because they are establishing new and effective clusterings of city and household functions. New services now fuse public and private life, suggesting new types of urban environment that are integral to changing social trends throughout the world and are likely to continue to do so into the next century.

Encouragingly, *Common Place* shows how a whole city could be seen to be involved in a design process, but it is hard to tell exactly who was being targeted by its planning concerns as the facilities proposed were often fixed to an anonymous time and drawing scale. Can planners today, continue to plan in large-scale isolation of new attitudes and approaches to, for example, product design and leasing, micro-economics and care? The new facilities and services intended for use by the older user, both unemployed and self-employed, offer much to planners wanting to incorporate the social changes that are beginning to affect cities and their growth; illustrating the new ways we work, play and care for each other. The smallest of details, equipment and skills which already exist in every home, if not house, can be catered for or even matched as they inevitably change over generations, but there are few flexible plans and smaller scales of analysis showing this.

Since the Second World War the pace of change in the way we use cities has accelerated and is likely to continue exponentially. *Common Place* could benefit from looking into how cities remain serviceable using sustainable permanence *and* flexibility over a specifically extended period. As individuals gain access to more efficient services, we are evolving under emerging, and as yet unknown, technological and social changes, demanding more adaptable designs, so that planners can be responsive to peoples' changing demands. In a 21st century likely to be marked by rapid and fundamental changes, trying to establish facilities for people and their relationships in cities means more disciplines face scenarios never encountered before, and environmental service providers/designers have to rely on more personal and proactive responses. What is needed are more interdisciplinary crossovers than ever before, so that deeper understandings, no matter how fantastic, can structure the diversifying analysis of what we shall need from our cities.

Mark Titman

DIGITAL PERSPECTIVES

CAD RENDERED IMAGE COMPETITION 1997
RIBA Student Gallery
September-October 1997

LEFT: Christian Groothuizen, 'Centre Point urban village', rendered computer image, 1997; RIGHT: James Gott, 'Dreaming of an Unthinkable Architecture', rendered computer image, 1997

Last July, UK students took up the challenge to produce an A3 computer-rendered image that proved their ability and imagination to push the boundaries of Computer Aided Design (CAD). The brief was purposely vague, requiring an image of the proposal, with no further development required or desired, offering the opportunity to produce a design that wasn't necessarily a building placed on a site, or governed by spatial limitations, context, gravity and regulations.

Indeed, the competition allowed participants to question the current definitions of 'paper' and 'real' architecture; highlighting the continuous debate in architectural schools on whether student projects should be buildable or conceptual. A virtual space allows users to realise either. As the winner James Gott said:

We would be entering a reality not unlike that of the lucid dreamer's. For virtual environments need not conform to all our perceived physical laws, they may be superimposed one on another infinitely, in this way creating spaces of a complexity that is inconceivable. By liberating the designers from physically building environments we can thus transcend the limitations of conceptual thought.

Other competitors preferred to use the possibilities of CAD technology to represent realistically a scheme which a student could never dream of constructing for many years. The potential to make things look slick and photogenic, fudging the surroundings, is another aspect of the power of computer imaging. In fact, the modelling consultants Hayes Davidson have lead the way in computer-generated photo-realism, producing images so 'real' that it is nearly an anticlimax to see the building in the reality!

Recent developments in special effects have transformed our enjoyment of many films. Perhaps we should expend similar energies in fulfilling our desire for architecture with virtual projects, and save money and resources in the building of our physical environment. If we can see and enjoy these newly created virtual spaces, we might be more willing to reuse and refurbish our existing buildings. However, where there is a need to build, then the potential for CAD to produce a building which is understandable to a client, and allows for changes to be made before a slab has been cast, is clear.

Warren Whyte

CONTEMPORARY MUSEUMS

DEREK WALKER ASSOCIATES, HALL OF STEEL, ROYAL ARMOURIES MUSEUM, LEEDS

Architectural Design

CONTEMPORARY MUSEUMS

OPPOSITE: GÜNTER ZAMP KELP, THE NEANDERTHAL MUSEUM, METTMANN, GERMANY
ABOVE: ALESSANDRO AND FRANCESCO MENDINI, GRONINGER MUSEUM, GRONINGEN, THE NETHERLANDS

ACADEMY EDITIONS • LONDON

Acknowledgements

We would like to express our gratitude to those who have contributed to this issue of *Architectural Design*, many of whom were present at the Academy Forum which was held at the Royal Academy of Arts, London, on 15 June 1996. We would also like to thank all those who have kindly allowed us to reproduce material for publication, including Nicholas Serota and Thames and Hudson, who granted us permission to publish an extract from *Experience of Interpretation: The Dilemma of Museums of Modern Art*, published in 1996. The majority of comments on page 96 are from the symposium on New Museology in 1991.

Photographic Credits: all material is courtesy of the authors and architects unless otherwise stated. Attempts have been made to locate the sources of all photographs to obtain full reproduction rights, but in the very few cases where this process has failed to find the copyright holder, our apologies are offered.
Richard Davies *pp1, 90-91*; Bruno Delamain *pp68-71*; E&S *p58*; Scott Frances/Esto *pp34-37*; Studio Hollein/Arch Sina Baniahmad *pp46-53*; Ariel Huber *p13*; Charles Jencks *pp8-11*; Masayosi Kato *pp84-85*; Søren Robert Lund *pp80-81*; Yoshiharu Matumura *p82 below, 51*; Nakasaka & Partners inc *p82 above, 83, 87*; Tomio Ohashi *pp54-57, 59*; Michael Reisch *pp2, 26*; R Richter/Architekturphoto *cover, p6, 25, 34, 36-41, 78*; John Stoel *pp35, 42 below left*; Nigel Young *pp54-59*.

Front cover: Søren Robert Lund, Arken Museum of Modern Art, Copenhagen, Denmark
Inside covers: Detail from an exhibit at the Royal Armouries Museum, Leeds

EDITOR: Maggie Toy
PRODUCTION EDITOR: Ramona Khambatta
ART EDITOR: Alex Young

First published in Great Britain in 1997 by *Architectural Design*,
42 LEINSTER GARDENS, LONDON W2 3AN

A division of John Wiley & Sons Ltd,
Baffins Lane, Chichester, West Sussex PO19 IUD

ISBN: 0-471-97738-1

The Publishers and Editor do not hold themselves responsible for the opinions expressed by the writers of articles or letters in this magazine
Copyright of articles and illustrations may belong to individual writers or artists
Architectural Design Profile 130 is published as part of
Architectural Design Vol 67 11-12 /1997
Architectural Design Magazine is published six times a year and is available by subscription

Distributed to the trade in the United States of America by
NATIONAL BOOK NETWORK INC, 4720 BOSTON WAY, LANHAM, MARYLAND, 20706

Printed and bound in Italy

Contents

ARCHITECTURAL DESIGN PROFILE No 130
CONTEMPORARY MUSEUMS

EDITORIAL
MAGGIE TOY

The building of a new museum is a daunting but extraordinarily challenging task for an architect today. The contemporary museum is a place with a multiplicity of functions, which must combine traditional roles of interpreting and conserving a wide range of artefacts with requirements for large-scale retail areas, complex new technologies and the circulation needs of ever-growing numbers of the museum-going public. All this must be achieved without compromising the sense of calm and contemplation necessary for a serious encounter with the works exhibited. Art is often forced to compete with the space in which it is exhibited and is reduced to decoration in the process.

The museum is a powerful cultural nexus, offering a mirror to how a society sees itself, as well as being a symbol of commercial and cultural achievement to the outside world. Frank Gehry in connection with his recently completed Guggenheim Museum in Bilbao – featured extensively in AD *New Science = New Architecture* Profile 129 – calls this 'iconic presence'. With the decline in organised religion, Sunday has for many people ceased to involve church; the new cathedrals are the shopping malls and the museums, the latter combining family entertainment, self-improvement and retail therapy. The architect must provide for all these often highly contradictory roles, summarised by Charles Jencks as a heady mixture of 'culture and speculation, spirituality and glamour, self-improvement and power'.

In the explosion of museum building we have witnessed in the last part of this century, the old precedents of monumental building have become obsolete as the desire to democratise the image of the museum has resulted in the development of a potent new building type. Up to the middle of this century a museum was a place of learning, in which notions of cultural dominance were reinforced visually through a severe and often intimidating approach to building. The museum now has to represent a much more welcoming, all embracing image, as it can no longer afford to present a single establishment view of society and its history but must now reflect a diversity of cultures and expectations. Contemporary museum architecture's most vital task is to communicate to the widest possible audience the breadth of collections and accessibility of learning facilities.

The theme of communication was vigorously discussed at the Academy Forum 'Spectacular Contradictions: The Museum in the 1990s', held at the Royal Academy of Arts, London, in June 1996. Debate centred around two recent, highly contrasting and equally successful projects, the new Groninger Museum in The Netherlands and the Royal Armouries Museum in Leeds. Both buildings have attracted huge numbers of visitors to collections which could be said to be of marginal appeal. The architectural richness of the Groninger Museum, described by Peter Cook as, 'on a knife edge sometimes between kitsch and brilliance' becomes an art-object in itself. It is a place which does not need to be validated by a display and many feel that it adds lustre to a somewhat piecemeal collection, which can be considered a dangerous course to take. By way of contrast the architecture of the Royal Armouries Museum takes a less dominant role and is designed purely to serve the collection but through its theatrical use of displays it serves to bring artefacts alive in the imagination of the viewer. As Guy Wilson puts it, he wants people to feel the same exhilaration they might feel coming out of a Shakespearean play.

In a previous issue of *Architectural Design* (New Museums, Profile No 94), we examined extensions to existing institutions such as the Sackler Galleries at the Royal Academy and the extension to London's National Gallery by Venturi/Scott Brown. This explored notions of stylistic integration between new extensions and their historical setting as well as the relationship between the architecture of the museum and its contents. As the obsession for museums has developed so the need for new buildings has increased and in this volume we present a series of diverse projects which have been developed from concept to completion.

Many of these museums form the centrepiece of major urban regeneration schemes. Hans Hollein's Guggenheim is situated in a previously run down area of Vienna. Its insertion into the urban fabric is intended to provide a cultural focus which will bring much more than artefacts and their viewers to this particular location. Renzo Piano's staggering tanker-shaped New Metropolis National Science and Technology Centre is 'moored' in the former dock area of Amsterdam, far enough away to be uninhibited by the architectural traditions of the city centre and a vital part of the revitalisation of that area. Another scheme which has also drawn together a fragmented city structure is Richard Meier's Museum of Modern Art in Barcelona; happening upon the Museum through narrow streets gives an unpredicted pleasure. Gehry's Guggenheim, which forms part of an extensive building campaign in the Basque country's largest city, Bilbao, is not only an attempt to introduce new investment into the area but also a symbol of Basque identity and self-confidence.

Designers and curators of the present day museum have undergone much consideration re-positioning their architecture to meet the new demands but, as many of the projects discussed in Clare Melhuish's essay testify, the 'iconic' power of the museum has never been stronger. Despite its new-found public image of diversity, democracy, pluralism and desire to appeal to a extensive audience, the museum's inextricable links with politics and perceived financial power seem clearer than ever.

Renzo Piano Building Workshop, New Metropolis National Science and Technology Center, Amsterdam

British Museum, London, pediment – the progress of civilisation leads to Britain, Robert Smirke, 1823-47

THE CONTEMPORARY MUSEUM

CHARLES JENCKS

The museum in the 1990s is an old lady suddenly turned into an oversexed teenager: she is pushed and pulled every way by hormones, exams and attractive, rich men on the horizon – promising everything, including ruin. Who can resist the opportunities and danger of this new, young thing? Curators, boards of directors, art investors, even artists, are all pulled in by the heady mixture of culture and speculation, spirituality and glamour, self-improvement and power. The contemporary museum is a spectacular contradiction of old requirements and new, mutant opportunities. Curators and architects will have to rethink this building type which now offers them unique, synergetic possibilities.

There are six principal roles it now plays, which are sometimes contradictory but potentially a source of refreshing contrast. From the past it inherits two main roles.

1. To *preserve and memorialise* artefacts and events. The role of the museums on the Acropolis was to remind the Athenians of their key victories over the Persians and citizens of Caryae. Hence the Caryatid porch on the Erechtheum; hence the parking lot of statues that surrounded the Parthenon; hence the museum inside the Propylaea – all these spaces and surfaces were filled with artefacts of tribute. The ancient museum held up ideals of nationhood and beauty for emulation. The temple and museum had overlapping roles, anticipating the 19th-century 'museum as cathedral' and a second main function.

2. To *educate and reaffirm* values. The museum was an active place of indoctrination and its educational function simply grew until, by the 19th century, it had taken on a quasi-scientific role in such places as the Louvre and the British Museum. At the beginning of the century these institutions had been repositories of knowledge often based on conquest. Napolean and the founders of the British Museum conveyed a double message with their collections: we have conquered the earth, and the objects shown here justify our claims as the true inheritors of historical destiny. Just as Darwinian evolution progresses from ape to man, so global history progresses from the Egyptians and Greeks to us. The collection and succession of styles had this implicit message, all the more powerful for being suggested rather than stated.

The pediment over the British Museum, with its female divinity of Britain, sweetly portrays this idea of cumulative progress. Its Ionic columns and proportions directly recall those of the Erechtheum, and inside the Museum an actual Caryatid has been taken from this Greek original. So the double message is sent: 'according to Vitruvius the Greeks portrayed the women of Caryae on their Erechtheum porch to teach them a lesson against rebellion; and now that we own a Caryatid, and the splendours of Greek and Rome, we summarise Western culture'.

To educate with 'the best that is thought and felt' through the ages was the elevated role of culture; a role which, as Matthew Arnold pointed out, was beginning to replace religion. This led directly to the third emergent function of the 1850s.

3. The *museum as substitute cathedral*, with culture and art as ersatz religions. Arnold may have believed that art makes a poor religion, but that has not stopped its new sacral role taking over in a post-Christian West. One cannot discuss the new functions of the museum without putting them in the context of the decline of Christianity and other religions, and the rise of the art market and mass culture.

The spectacular fact of these spectacular changes in spectacle is that no one asked for them, no one designed them, and few saw them coming. It is true that the avant-garde, which trumpets its beginning in the 1820s, also sees its role as 'the new priest' of a secular society. Artists today often act like priests (without portfolio), and they *do* have a remaining spiritual function – to symbolise the creativity of the universe and its uncanny surprise – but they make bad theologians, and they don't have a public creed. Nevertheless, the public now flocks to both old avant-garde – Cézanne – and new – Damien Hirst – as if they hope to find spiritual nourishment. Who can blame the museum for providing the equivalent of a mystical epiphany when the church has lost its cultural credibility?

It may have taken 100 years for the cliché 'museum as cathedral' to take root but its presence was already well established by the time Alfred Waterhouse had designed the Natural History Museum in the shape of a Romanesque Cathedral – with real and angelic animals decorating the skyline, and dinosaurs down the nave. Nonetheless, this third function, the spiritual role, is *not* publicly addressed by museum curators, nor is there any agreed iconography or programmatic acknowledgement by the museum which would take it on. There is a vague notion of

Natural History Museum, London – the iconography and layout of a Romanesque Cathedral, Alfred Waterhouse, 1881

providing atmosphere, a sense of awe and the aura of unique-ness (put in question, it is often claimed, by the age of mechanical reproduction). There is a feeling that museums should provide a hushed, reverential tone. But the only explicit convention is that museums display their treasured objects as if they were religious icons – highlighted on pedestals, behind glass, and carefully removed from profane contamination.

This removal partly conflicts with the next main function that grew in the 1960s and exploded in the 1980s:

4. The museum as a *place of entertainment* for the whole family. 'More Americans', it is often said, 'go to museums than go to football games'. More Britons go to cultural institutions than to sporting events. This mass cultural fact has dramatic consequences for the way museums are designed and experienced, for it means – like the entrance to the new Sainsbury Wing at the National Gallery – that the front door must be (as Robert Venturi said) like a stadium entrance, a 'vomitorium', leading directly to an information kiosk, shopping mall and 'spaghetti junction' of pedestrian superhighways leading away from it.

'Vomitorium' at the Sainsbury Wing. Because of its mass culture role, Robert Venturi made this comparison to a stadium entrance, 1986

Needless to say, there is a spectacular contradiction between jamming three million people through these vomitoriums every year and the quiet, spiritual dialogue between individual and icon. Previously, one used to enter up steps into a pure, classical world: now backpackers flood off the bus to snatch as many views per second as they can over the backpacker in front. The church used to handle this contradiction between mass pilgrimage and private worship with side chapels and a walk around the crypt; most museums today handle it with an art store in front and a temple atmosphere behind.

A place of entertainment for the whole family leads to the kind of organisational patterns that Disney has pioneered for large numbers: the crowd management barriers, the emphasis on interactive display and dramatic lighting. Another consequence of this, which is closely related, is the next role, which also grew in the 1960s:

5. The *blockbuster exhibition and shopping precinct*. Both of these new, mutant roles can be seen where they originated: at the Metropolitan Museum in New York and the new Louvre (underground) in Paris. The facts of large numbers, large shopping facilities, large-scale marketing are intertwined with the blockbuster exhibition, the gold of Tutankhamun, the gold of China, the gold of Mexico and Peru – people's love for spectacle and profit, or lucre on display. The process began, as Robert Hughes pointed out, when the Met spent $2.3 million on Rembrandt's *Aristotle Contemplating the Bust of Homer*, and put a red velvet rope around it to distinguish it from all other Rembrandts.[1] By the mid-60s the *new* art market had been launched and fixed as a big business enterprise through the Times-Sotheby Art Indexes. These, for the first time, showed how art could mimic the rising fortunes of Ford or IBM, and the graphs rising towards Mount Everest convinced corporations, and Japanese in search of Van Gogh, that £20 to £30 million was not a bad investment for a scarce item.

The £1 million, avant-garde masterpiece has become another cliché and self-fulfilling prophecy; today one does not blink when a Mark Rothko goes for over £2 million, a Jackson Pollock or Jasper Johns for more than £10 million. The mass media keeps reminding us of the figures and thus we have become used to another kind of spectacular contradiction: Old Master Dadaists, collectible Nihilists, SuperRich Dropouts – the graffiti artists like Jean-Michel Basquiat who seek to rival the Rockefellers.

Robert Hughes traces the developing art market right to the site of the conference – to the Royal Academy and Sir Joshua Reynolds' desire to establish artists in power and pocket. Hughes quotes the opposing views of the time: William Blake (who said that Sir Joshua was invented to depress art: 'where any view of money exists') asserted, like the spiritually motivated purist he was, 'art cannot be carried on'. Samuel Johnson put the opposite case for culture: 'No man but a blockhead ever wrote, except for money' . . . and Johnson proved statistically more accurate than Blake. Money helps the muse and museum, to a degree, and when dished out in the right manner. For Titian it was motivating, but when it is thrown at a few young priests of the avant-garde – like Julian Schnabel – it can lock them into a stereotype, just as it does any other corporate mass-producer.

The influence of the art market on the museum is to turn it into a place of glamour and spectacle. When Burlington House became the Royal Academy it used the classical imagery of the palace and country house as a backdrop. These rooms are meant to enhance the glamour of the display and displayers in much the same way as the state rooms of Buckingham Palace. However, with the art opening becoming the new ritual for self-display, the museum mutated – as the Guggenheim Museum in New York so deftly shows – into a strong, white background against which men in black tie and women in colour can be seen rising, descending, from afar and close up. The implication? One goes to an opening not to choose a spiritual painting but a rich partner.

Now all museums must be conceived as a theatre for this ritual. There is another pressure, related to this and the avant-garde, which has a somewhat contradictory effect on the museum:

6. The *site of the culture industry*, the place where thousands of artists, art professionals and media amplifiers must work. In New York City alone, in 1982 (the last statistics I have) there were 14,000 artists with gallery affiliations; in America in 1984, according to Hughes, 35,000 painters, sculptors, critics and art historians graduated from art school. Such numbers indicate that there ought to be many more great painters alive than in the Renaissance, since 15th-century Florence had only about 70,000 citizens.

However, what it has led to is not more good artists but, as Tolstoy pointed out, many more art-explainers, art-expositors, art-swindlers, art-dealers and artistic movements. In a capitalist market, they say of successful products: 'it is the different that makes a difference – that sells'. This extreme differentiation, caused by the great numbers making and buying art, means that the museum must become the nerve centre of the culture industry. It has to educate and, above all, authenticate.

When parking in downtown America, one has a parking voucher 'validated', so one does not have to pay. In America when an art dealer has a potentially hot artist, he takes the artist to the local museum and gets him validated with a show – or, better yet, Christies, and the validation of a sale price.

Economic validation is what an exhibition at New York's Museum of Modern Art confers on any avant-garde artist or architect, which is why Philip Johnson and others control, so assiduously, the corridors and white display rooms of that Vatican. This leads the museum on to the roles I have mentioned – place of memory, education, religious experience, entertainment and shopping – but to becoming a Bank of England, Stock Market and university, all in one. The culture industry must work here to see who is on top, or who gets on top. At the Royal Academy it is Norman Rosenthal's self-proclaimed job, or, at the Tate, what Nicholas Serota admits is necessary. Stocks must be kept high and for that to happen in the complex, post-modern world of international quotations, the shows must be changed constantly and with acuity. That is not possible unless the museum has a vast structure and space for the culture industry.

Juxtaposing the types

These six functions by no means exhaust the range of new roles which are emerging – for instance, the job of being an information net that can beam flat and sterile simulacra into anyone's home. But they do show that the museum is mutating in ways no one predicted, or even wanted. To reflect adequately these fast

changes one has to respond with a light touch, like a surfer making split-second decisions which will have sudden and long-term implications. One obvious possibility is that the contradictory functions increase the pleasure and depth of a museum and make it into a key new building type. Frans Haks, and his four architects led by Alessandro Mendini, have created a successful system of differences at the Groninger Museum in Holland. This juxtaposition of spaces, moods and structure brings out the qualities of different periods of art, and refreshes the experience with contrasting views of the city and water.

Derek Walker and Guy Wilson, in their presentation of the Royal Armouries Museum in Leeds, also spoke of their commitment to portraying difference. The Display Design Consultants were to take the lead in design and thus make every display dictate the architecture around it. The result, however, looks more like the neutral background of 'the museum as warehouse' than the heterogeneous museum in Groningen – the consequence, no doubt, of one architect designing the whole. Wilson spoke of the building task as a 'museum of human violence' since killing and weaponry were the main attractions (aside from a few displays of Peace Movements). 'The Hall of Steel' with its serried ranks of spikes and swords, glorified these armaments as does any castle – by turning them into Op Art repetitions. Derek Walker portrayed the opposite meanings of war – glory and horror – in the materials and general treatment. Now that there are several Holocaust Museums, and quite a few war museums, this mixed genre is beginning to be understood for what it is: another spectacular contradiction. It is a pity the oppositions were not faced and dramatised in Leeds as they were in Groningen.

Lucio Passarelli, in his museum designs and his discussion of the new Louvre, brought out two of the main contradictory

Museum as juxtaposed pavilions – Frans Haks asked Alessandro Mendini to work with other architects to create this system of difference at the Groninger Museum, Groningen, Holland, 1994

requirements – what he called the 'Pre- and Post-Museums'. These areas, projected for the Vatican, are elaborate entrances and exits (even mounting three storeys), places where one queues and shops before the experience and then, afterwards, memorialises and shops again. The methods of crowd control have long been developed by the Vatican, and perfected by Disney, and they are now turning into celebratory areas in their own right. If this trend continues then one day the carnivalesque queue-architecture will be more exciting than the museum itself.

This problem of the setting taking over from the art or, as Robert Maxwell put it, stage-set architecture becoming dominant, became apparent in the 1980s. Disney's Entertainment Architecture, the name they gave to their approach of exaggerating the theme in the theme park, may enhance the role of art or smother it. The related question was raised several times: how can the work of art recapture its lost aura – especially in the age of electronic reproduction and CD-ROM?

One response, claimed Paul Finch, was to go underground as Hollein's museums have done, as if to root their objects in an archaeological site. This *does* appear to be a trend against ephemera, albeit a minor one. In fact, it has been argued by Andreas Huyssen that the prevalence of museum building today is a deep psychological response to the ephemeralisation of life by the media.[2] People go to museums for grounding and orientation, because the order of the past, as signified by the collection, has a permanence and relevance for the future. In TS

Eliot's idea of tradition, works of art and culture form an ideal order which helps steer the individual.

If this is true then the consequences for museums in a global civilisation are profound. They will have to make clear, at one and the same time, the plurality of local traditions, national trends and global movements. Again there will be an argument for an architecture of contrast and juxtaposition which the Groninger Museum makes – with the addition of a global or universal thread. As to the latter, Daniel Libeskind's proposed addition to the Victoria & Albert Museum is a good exemplar. It is made up from a spiral of universal 'fractiles'; that is, fractal shapes of tiles which spin upwards in plan, volume and detail. These mimic the fractals of nature and those of the tile collection inside the V&A – universal ordering principles which Islamic culture has always featured.

What then is the museum of spectacular contradiction? To design and run it takes completely opposing skills; to make it successful as theatre and fund-raising require different temperaments; to make it a cathedral and shop require different sides of the brain, or different brains altogether. Even art and architecture can fight it out. To make a virtue of all these conflicts takes a clear understanding that they really exist. If inventively combined, the disparate parts may provide just the kind of experience to cure museum fatigue and make this building type a fitting centre for the global city of contradictions. The museum as cathedral might then become more than a convenient cliché.

Notes

1 Robert Hughes, 'Art and Money', 1984: reprinted in *Nothing if not Critical*, Alfred Knopf (New York), 1990, pp387-404. Hughes makes some very interesting points about the way the art market has changed over the last 300 years and its effect on

the way art is produced and perceived.
2 Andreas Huyssen, *Twilight Memories, Marking Time in a Culture of Amnesia*, Routledge (New York, London), 1995.

The glory of killing machines – Hall of Steel at the Royal Armouries Museum, Leeds, Derek Walker Associates, 1996

Universal fractiles – the spiral of self-similar order that emerges at the proposed addition to the Victoria & Albert Museum, London, Daniel Libeskind, 1996

ACADEMY FORUM

SPECTACULAR CONTRADICTIONS

The Museum in the 1990s

The following extracts are taken from the Academy Forum discussion held at the Royal Academy of Arts, London, on 15 June 1996, which preceded the Annual Academy Architecture Lecture, 'The Architect as Seismograph', given by Hans Hollein.

Paul Finch: The subject of museums takes us back to 1991, where in the Royal Academy we held a symposium on the new museology and took the opportunity to ponder the way in which architects were now relating to artists – or not, in terms of the sort of spaces that they made for them. When we were planning this series we had a working title which was 'shop, pray and go', or possibly 'shop, pray and exit', which was a reference to the way in which museums and galleries seem to be increasingly about circulation, about the sale of retail items related to the particular cultural activity taking place within them. The specific role of the new museums and galleries in London, whether they are brand new or extensions to the existing structure, is being seen in an entirely new light; for example, in terms of the volumes of people they are having to cater for and the types of exhibitions they are showing.

This afternoon we will have two brief presentations by Professor Stephen Bann, and by Guy Wilson and Derek Walker, preceded by some preliminary comments from Charles Jencks. So without further ado – Charles Jencks.

Charles Jencks: Thank you. I want to say a few words about the title, 'Spectacular Contradictions: the Museum in the 1990s' to set the framework, theory and history that I hope we delve into this afternoon. I think it is generally felt that the museum today is evolving so fast that one could speak of a mutation – a mutation in this extraordinary building type which may have origins in Greece. In the populous of the acropolis there was a museum, the Parthenon, which itself can be considered a museum surrounded by a parking lot of things discarded there to increase in value, such as trophies and devotional objects.

So we have more than a 2,000-year-old history of this museum type, which in the late 19th century starts to take off in another way and in the 1960s and 1970s becomes very much tied to the art market and its explosion, with all sorts of implications. Then, along with the blockbuster and the museum as a shopping mall, it mutates again and becomes a place where the culture industry gathers; that is, the thousands and thousands of intermediaries between the artists and the public.

The basic argument is that this type is evolving simultaneously in different directions: directions which I think Cedric Price refers to in his contribution to the handout sheet, which summarises maybe 10 or so views of what is happening today. It is this evolution, which is without control – or out of control – that we are exploring today. When such evolutions happen it is of course possible that there are great opportunities for synergy and for mixing functions, roles and values that did not exist previously. These have clearly changed since the 1980s when everybody

confirmed that the museum was now some kind of cathedral or temple in a post-Christian or declining religious society. The question is how we can pull together in one person – the minds of the curator, the architect, the museum director or the board of trustees – this hydra-headed, quickly evolving animal. This is the background for opening the debate.

Stephen Bann, who will start off the debate, studied in Cambridge in the 1960s. He is now Professor at the School of Art and Image Studies and directs the interdisciplinary Centre for Modern Cultural Studies in the University of Kent. So he is very well equipped to deal with these contradictions. Stephen.

Stephen Bann: Thank you Charles. I am perhaps going to take the slightly less strenuous path than the analysis of contradictions. I will certainly be concerned with the idea of the spectacular but what I want to talk about, which I think fits very much into the same way of thinking, is the museum in and as dialogue – that is to say, the sense in which, quite apart from the kind of morphology of the development of museums that Charles has just alluded to, it can be seen as a discursive and dialogic space. This is perhaps not its primary function but it is certainly one of its most important in establishing connections with earlier modes of display and spectacle; indeed, in that sense, it has an in-built historical dimension, even when concerned with the exhibition and display of wholly contemporary modes of representation.

What I want to talk about in particular is the way in which a contemporary museum can in a certain sense fulfil a sort of historicist project developed within museum culture and historical culture generally. First of all with reference to that amazing melting pot of historical culture: the period of Romanticism. It is almost 20 years, I think, since I began to analyse what has fascinated me ever since: the initial circumstances of the setting up of the Hôtel de Cluny as the Museum de Cluny in Paris in the late 1820s to 1830s by Du Sommerard.

Collected pieces of very diverse provenance were arranged in rooms that were intended to simulate the atmosphere of a previous period, such as the Salle de François Premier. It was here that I think for the first time, because the conditions simply didn't exist before, there was a couple of suits of armour sitting opposite one another in a window embrasure 'playing' chess; likewise, in the chapel of the Museum de Cluny, the presence of a cowled figure, in fact a mannequin, standing beside the altar.

Apparently, if we are to judge by contemporary accounts, this caused some very diverse opinions and states of extreme shock when visitors discovered that the mannequin was not a real person. Having been myself, only last weekend, to see the Royal Armouries Museum in Leeds, it does interest me that the strategic use of the suit of armour is, one could say, the primary trope of the Royal Armouries Museum in obtaining the recreative procedure.

Of course, to amplify a romantic trope – that of lived life – is something that can be done with much more impoverished material. One of the museums that has impressed me most over the last year or two has been the quite extraordinary, new Museum of Sydney. This is hardly more than a slice of almost transparent construction on the facade of a high-rise building not far from the harbour, incorporating only a reference to the ground plan of the original government house. In this condition of extreme transparency, modern Sydney is vitrified as you are offered individual narratives of alternative lifestyles – the servant and the master and so on – lived at the time of the original settlement in Sydney.

There is a remarkable system of draws with tiny objects which are derived archaeologically from this very recent settlement. I am told that visitors stop, on average, as much as two hours in order to see the magic of these little curiosities emerging out of their metal trays. Also, to compensate again for what is a settlement that has left no trace, you experience an inventive use of sound which permeates the museum, floats around it and establishes a continuous kind of background dialogue in which the spectator can intervene.

What I have called a dialogue in this sense is, of course, not something that has to be necessarily based on a historical relationship, a historical rapport. You will be learning much more later on this afternoon about the Groninger Museum in Groningen and so I won't say much about this at the moment. But I will say that the traditional assumption, as you approach the museum from the station, is that it is out of tune with this wonderful old Dutch town. However, while walking around Groningen with a local guide, I learned that not very long ago the church spire of the most prominent building was painted a very distinctive colour: a sort of mustard yellow. It was explained to me that throughout Groningen this colour was picked up by people who were using it for their front door, or it was applied in other ways.

Here was a sense of a kind of will towards spectacle and display, expressed by the collective identification with this spectacular central church, which I think is also evident in the external display of the Coop Himmelblau wing of the Groninger Museum. Visually, it is not entirely unlike the new project for the Victoria & Albert Museum in London, where the architects relate the material claddings to the V&A collection. This is another kind of dialogue: a dialogue between the external appearance and the internal holdings; also, a dialogue with the particular kind of expertise which the museum staff see themselves embodying in their collections.

Finally, I want to say just one or two words about the work of Hans Hollein. His preoccupation with light as well as the material of the museum space is something which I can't resist associating with the work of John Soane – although I have no idea whether there's any sort of direct connection with his work in Lincoln's Inn Fields or the Dulwich Picture Gallery, where the entry and reflection of light becomes, as it were, the primary theme which carries and binds together the otherwise heterogeneous array of materials which are placed on display. In the case of the Abteilberg Mönchengladbach museum, which houses a collection that is undoubtedly one of the most daring but successful of modern collections – the Marx collection – his particular use of space and light is remarkable in the way in which it actually provides such an appropriate and differentiating context for such a collection. The image I am left with is of light issuing through the little dome, illuminating the plaster of Paolini's Venus. I think this sums up the dialogue of the contemporary museum with the classical tradition and with so many great museums of the past. Thank you.

Paul Finch: Thank you very much Stephen. We're going to move straight on to something that you yourself referred to which is the Royal Armouries Museum in Leeds designed by Derek Walker, who is best known in this country for being Chief Architect and Planner of Milton Keynes, which is surviving pretty well I think. He has come very much into the public eye with the creation of this new museum and the presentation will be made with Guy Wilson who is the Master of Armouries and, I read, the 18th person to hold this title since the 13th century. There was much controversy when the decision was taken to move this collection from The Tower of London to Leeds but it has had a fantastic popular reception.

Guy Wilson: Before handing over to Derek I just want to say a few words as a museum person – if you like, the client for this museum. I am a practical person not a theorist, so when the opportunity arose to create a new museum we looked at it in a very practical way. What is it that our museum was there to do? That was one of the reasons why we wanted a new museum in the first place.

We were set up by an Act of Parliament which tells us what we are there to do and fundamentally we have various duties, the most important of which is that of displaying and interpreting our collections for the public in a way which will interest them in the subject. Now everything that we do as a museum should be directed one way or another towards that. Therefore, in creating a new museum, or new displays, we were looking at making our displays overtly more popular and interesting to more people. That is why the government pays us money.

My own personal view of museum displays – past, present and future – is that perhaps we have responded to our educational role in the past with more intellectual vigour than emotion. A lot of museums, therefore, have failed to inspire an interest in a large number of their visitors, who respond more naturally to an emotional approach to subjects than an intellectual one. One of the things that I said to Derek when we started the process was that I would like people to come out of the museum with the same feeling as that which they would have experienced from a wonderful production, such as a Shakespearean play. Why shouldn't people come out of museums with that sort of feeling? Some do now, but not enough.

Therefore, in looking at how we were going to design our new museum we were looking at bringing in all sorts of modern ways of communicating an interest in what at first sight seems to be a strange and obscure subject – arms and armour. However many books you have about however many subjects, arms and armour probably is not one of the foremost interests. Yet arms and armour exist because of one very human factor and that is human violence. An arms and armour museum is a museum of human violence and the violence in the world around human beings. It is a profoundly interesting, important, disturbing and continuing subject. We are therefore not just a history museum but a museum of the present and future of human violence. The challenge was how to convey that in a museum and how to use all the different techniques.

As a practical person, I was aware that not many national museums have been built recently in this country. Very few of us in the museum profession, therefore, ever have the opportunity to be involved in creating an entirely new museum and so when we start, we don't know what we're doing. There is less knowledge about the particular requirements of museums and art galleries than in various other types of building, which suggested to us that if we were to make best use of this unique opportunity to create a new museum we needed to go about it very carefully. We needed to develop a relationship with an architect which would enable us to express what we wanted and allow the architect to understand what we were, what our collections were, what they could do and what we wanted to do with them. So the collections became fundamental to the whole process.

The brief included a section about the importance of the displays: 'The building is a vessel which contains the displays and allows them to succeed. The display must dominate every element, area and floor of the museum. Even when not in the galleries the visitors must be aware of the collections by sympathetic design. The Royal Armouries is determined that its new museum will be designed properly so that it provides a fitting home for the collection of the museum. In order to achieve this, the needs of the collection and its display must dominate the design of the building.' Our way of reconciling the various objectives, such as interior design and display design, and the holistic approach to the building, was to appoint Derek Walker himself not only as architect but as the head of the whole display and design process, working for me.

Derek Walker: The fundamental aim of the design team was precisely what Guy has pointed out. The most important thing was that we had a great collection put together over a period of over 400 years which was going to be the generator of any building form that we were able to look at. It has never really been shown particularly well because much of it has been set within the Tower of London and much of it has been in storage. It has never really had the fundamental background to show the real quality of the individual pieces. As a museum that is constantly living – relating human violence, hunting, and so on – every subject heading had to be brought up to date.

One of the key elements of the building which we had discussed was the idea of going back to mass display in a very big way; something which had been very much a part of the Tower credentials during the 19th century but had not been done very much since that period of time. There are a lot of repetitive objects within the armouries store that we wished to display and it seemed to us that a Hall of Steel which could incorporate over 3,000 objects in a mass display was very much a central item of the building itself.

Externally, there was the need to re-enact a whole series of events and Guy scripted a whole series of demonstration performances both inside and outside the building, from tournament, falconry and birds of prey within the courtyard itself to a whole series of elements with backdrops within the museum. There is quite a considerable hunting collection within the museum itself and children – school children – are very much part of the day-to-day operation of the building. It is a place where ethnic exhibitions and large-scale military events take place; where, in fact, a whole series of around 43 films has been made, throughout the museum, covering all periods of history, many of them scripted by Guy Wilson and done superbly well by Yorkshire Television who are part of the main team.

The variety within each gallery is largely open display, closed display, some backdrops, which were basically 'ghosts' of individual objects. A whole series of models was made for the museum, animated with the works of arts and the reproductions. It is a museum where all elements come within the galleries:

static display, theatrical presentations and demonstrations. The idea is to use words, symbols and imagery to present the individual objects on display. Each gallery has a different kind of atmosphere and a different series of objectives. For example, the Self Defence Gallery is very low and uses very hard surfaces. It is very menacing and is largely about man's need to defend himself over the years.

One of the most priceless objects in the museum is the mask given to Henry VIII by the Emperor Maximilian: the horn helmet. This particular object, I think, sums up the chameleon nature of the museum. We tried desperately hard to follow the objectives of the Master of the Armouries and produce something that evolves around a collection, rather than a place into which one merely shoves a collection. What I have learnt, certainly over the last three years during this particular period, is that there are only two types of museums: the first is basically an art object in itself, which is constructed almost without due cognisance of a collection, or perhaps not for a particular collection, although perfectly legitimate. The second type is one that has to and should follow the collection, which is most important.

With regard to the Royal Armouries Museum, I had only seen many of the objects in draws when studying the collection. In my mind it is telling that a curator who had been with the museum for many years came to me after completion and said that he had never ever seen the collection before. The fact that we had managed to inspire this emotion in him was the highest possible praise that the design team as a whole could have had. Also, a child in a wheelchair felt that it had been one of the very few buildings that he had been able to get around properly and that he thought it was like having history told to him in a dream. Guy is probably right, in a sense, that emotion tends to govern a great deal of work and tends occasionally to transcend intellectual or theatrical ideas.

I think that what we have produced is a building which is exceedingly cheap: in square footage terms it is about 180,000 square feet per £20 million, which is fairly good. It is a dense building by the very nature of the collection which necessitated a kind of climatic condition and a servicing condition that was very demanding indeed. We have tried, within the plan-form and the movement through it, to bring the public to the outside of the building via a variety of oriole windows, so that in each gallery there is a place to stop and stare; to look out of the gallery itself. Unfortunately, we had to open it a little prematurely before it was finished because the Queen was going to Kentucky. Therefore, its daily opening has caused great problems in terms of getting the builders back to do the remedial work necessary to make it a decent building. Thank you.

Stephen Bann: What the Royal Armouries Museum is effectively, it seems to me, is a museum that actually narrates; one that actually places within a spatial display, types of explanation relating to human practices of a very widely disparate and discrepant kind. I was very interested actually to hear of all kinds of circumstances behind the building of the museum, which of course I didn't know when I went to see it. To return to my previous example, the Museum de Cluny, here effectively one had all these clues around the room. However, although in the 1820s people might have read the occasional Walter Scott novel, they would have had very little else to actually start them off thinking about the really different circumstances in which people in the 16th century lived. They were therefore experiencing something quite new, which was being brought into the consciousness by the particular paraphernalia of the collection.

I think that one can draw an analogy here with what is being done in a museum such as the Royal Armouries – appreciating, of course, the particular circumstances of our own highly technological civilisation, whose own narratives are almost word-perfect. What I would hope this museum does and what I think it does do, is to produce a kind of additional self-consciousness to that narrative dimension concerning situations of war, violence and hunting. The inclusion, for example, of the non-European forms of warfare and hunting is very important there. They form more than a mere appendage or annex to the central area.

The aspect that I find problematic about the museum concerns the use of references and representations. For example, some portraits are original, others are not, such as the *Battle of Pavia*, which is a reproduction but framed as an original picture. There are many framing devices which are necessary to establish, for example, the difference between a theatrical space and a space which is a 16th-century representation of a battle. The other personal problem, which is perhaps superficial but in others perhaps more deeply rooted, is to do with interactive mechanisms. Could one actually envisage oneself losing the Battle of Pavia if one was on the right side? We experiment through the interactive technique of configuring things differently. Although this is quite an interesting possibility, it is one that I am not sure I know how to deal with.

Guy Wilson: One of the reasons for the interactive side is to try and overcome the idea that history always had to be as it was. In so many of these battles the ebb and flow and final decision rested upon one particular tiny thing, or was not able to be deciphered, and so things could easily have gone the other way. There are various ways a battle could have been won or lost and it may help to make people understand that the thread of history is a very, very thin one. Yes, Catherine?

Catherine Cooke: When you talked about the theme of violence, what are actually the techniques that communicate this? My impression, when looking at everything, was almost a kind of virtual reality history and that although you talked about emotion, I thought we were really going to feel something about the passions of these soldiers and the confrontations and so on. Maybe it is science, but I felt less emotionally inflicted upon. What I was so interested in was what those things were made of and how this changes over time, so that people come away with some sense of time – the most important thing about museums, which is quite different from reading imagery.

Guy Wilson: We may be wrong, but my view of direct display of an artefact, of a gun or whatever, is actually that the emotion, the human interest, the story, the time, the value, comes from other things which you do. It is the use of sound, music, poetry, drama, films and all those sorts of things which are part of the experience when you go there. There are additional things which we hope make it different and offer an alternative experience for those who want such an experience. If you want to go around and just look at the objects you can do that.

Michael Compton: What we actually have to ask ourselves here is what is it that you would like to show in a museum and what is actually capable of being shown in a museum. I feel that the horror of the 1914 trenches or of the Holocaust, for example, make these unsuitable subjects for museums. You go to museums essentially to see objects which we have, for hundreds of years, been accustomed to think of as being beautiful. To get rid of that notion is extremely difficult. Therefore, we see a horseman not as an aggressive object but as an object with wonderful wrought armour. There are other means – films for instance – that can show horror much more successfully and therefore the contradictions in many museums are between the essential notion of the museum, which is to show real objects and the essence of the realness of those objects, and the emotions that we ascribe to those, which are very hard to disentangle from the object.

Derek Walker: I think that one of the reasons for making 43 films for this particular museum was the absolute need to be able to communicate precisely what Catherine is talking about. Anyone who has read Wilfred Owen and goes into the sights and sounds of war, which is one of the small theatres within the War Gallery, can hear two hours of the most extraordinary beautiful and moving things. You can't get this across in a slide or a discussion and it seems to me that the essence of the presentation of subject matter of this sort cannot be done without it being done in the most sensitive and direct way. In the Oriental Gallery, when you look at objects which are not automatically part of your everyday life and you see the absolute pristine beauty of a Japanese sword, and then you actually see what it can do, it is horrific – that is the curious thing of an object of exquisite beauty.

Paul Finch: Derek, can I raise the general point about the nature of the museum as a building type. It seems that you can't have a museum without a shop now; in fact, one of the first things in the brief for the Tate Gallery, Bankside, was the requirement to have retail areas. Now if you are looking at these building types, to what extent do you see them as essentially about the same sort of thing? It is actually simply the content that changes. I mean, to be fanciful for a moment, could one imagine the Royal Armouries Museum as a department store and Selfridges as a museum? And do we see with the sort of surface shopping centres, or out-of-town malls, a kind of different model that is more like a gallery model? Do you feel, in any sense, that you might be designing the same sort of thing?

Derek Walker: Well, you can convert a great railway station and make it into a passably good museum. It has been done, for example at the Musée d'Orsay in Paris. It depends on whether what you have is idiosyncratic. To design for paintings is very different than designing for objects and demands a totally different approach in every sense of the word. Guy was so positive in terms of the collection – in fact, the actual architecture coming out of the collection. Whether he was right or wrong I don't know. But it has worked in that sense: in that the objects do seem appropriately placed.

I don't like being logged into specific types because when we designed the shopping centre in Milton Keynes it was planned totally by every major shopping developer in the world – at the time, Aladdin's caves were the order of the day. You went into a darkened interior like the big French malls and never saw daylight until you came out. We introduced streets that were basically 'covered streets', which were ordinary main streets for a small town and put landscape in them, that's all. At that time it was a big deal because it wasn't happening.

Jeremy Melvin: I am very struck by the similarity in diagrammatic terms in the section of the Royal Armouries and of the conversion of Bankside Power Station to the Tate Gallery. The large public spaces in both buildings, although different in size, have quite similar functions. They are to do with getting the public into the museum building without necessarily forcing them to go and see the displays. This may have commercial implications for corporate hospitality, or for retail, or it may purely be a gesture of the improvement of public space in the city. If we are looking at the way a formal type might be evolving around the new museum that could possibly be a starting point.

I was trying to think why this might have occurred and something that Charles said right at the beginning set off a train of thought. He said that the Parthenon could be seen as a museum in the sense that it is instructive but it also combines public space with higher organisations or buildings to which access is restricted, and the combination of those is fundamental to the creation of some notion of Greek society: the control, the regulation of the way people behave in public.

I was wondering whether there was a connection between the way the Royal Armouries Museum and the Tate Gallery at Bankside are inviting public access, which is not necessarily to see the displays, but also controlling and ordering that in a particular way. This is, I think, generally to do with the workings of commerce, and the funding of museums.

Geoffrey Broadbent: I am very intrigued by the distinction that was made between objects that can be in a museum and what cannot be displayed. If I go to something called the National Gallery or the Tate Gallery I expect to see original paintings and sculptures by great artists with no question at all of any kind of reproduction. If I go to Leeds I will see both and I'm not sure I can tell the difference between the original weapon and the reproduction that is used in one of the sets. I think it is extraordinary to contemplate the limitations of all that.

Museums mean all those things. Some of them are proper galleries, in the sense of the National Gallery, and some are not: they are approaching Disney World really. I was horrified to go to the Science Museum a little while ago and see a demonstration of holograms. They used to have Naum Gabo's original hologram mechanism but now a reproduction is used to show how holograms work. It is great for the school parties to see how holograms work but there is another place to show these things. I wonder if you aren't teetering a bit on that edge too?

Guy Wilson: There is a tradition in social history museums certainly – not art museums – of using reproductions to illuminate a real object rather than relying simply upon the original. We have done no more than include more of those things and there are approximately 3,000 reproduction illustrations within the museum. They are kept separate from the real things which we display because when it is a real thing it is labelled so that people should be able to understand. Only in one of the displays – the Pavia display – do real pieces of armour and replica pieces of armour appear in the same integral whole. Otherwise, it is always all replica, or all not, as is tradition. We have tried, therefore, to keep things separate.

As to what is appropriate for a museum and what is not, I think it is for the user rather than the provider – whether it is the architect or museum person – to decide this. We are the guardians of the collection and we have the responsibility to interest people in it. In the end, it is the people out there who have to determine how we work and what we have to do to interest them in that collection. The danger with a lot of things is that we end up interesting people for interest's sake or to get more people to come in, rather than interesting them in the collection. That is where I would draw the distinction: that it must always be collection based, as we have tried to do and will continue to do so.

Paul Finch: I would like to read out an editorial I have written for next week. By reading it out I will be able to quote myself and therefore prove that what I have said was, in fact, history rather than fantasy on my part.

It is headed 'Museums, always on a Sunday' and it reads prophetically: 'A Royal Academy Symposium last Saturday discussed the way in which museums and galleries have changed their character in recent years under the title of "Spectacular Contradictions, Museums in the 90s". The working title of the event was the more flip "shop, pray and go" since it has now become apparent that temples of culture have replaced temples of religion as gathering places for social interaction, light – or not so light – shopping and as a Mecca for tourists and other visitors. That is why paintings in major institutions are said to be looked at by the average visitor for three seconds. All that is really needed are people movers to ensure that the seriously interested do not interfere with the fluid dynamic cultural experience of the majority.

'In this model of art replacing religion, which explains why so much activity takes place on a Sunday, the cultural validation of the trip is provided by the icons of religious life. Pilgrims gather at the shrine of St Cézanne, St Degas, St Rothko. Indulgences are purchased from the inevitable shops in the nave of the National Gallery, the Tate, the Victoria & Albert. Catalogues are bought instead of candles. Curators and critics act as Bishops and Deans. Prize-givings are feast days. Art students and those in theological colleges are learning their mantras of modernism and genuflecting to St Damien Hirst in his Jekyll and formaldehyde phase. There are prophets and heretics, visionaries and pariahists, the money changers are not turned out of the temple however, but ushered in to provide matching funding for the next lottery bid.

'The architectural consequences of all this are considerable. The museum and gallery increasingly resemble other building types in which circulation, ease of movement, display and purchase are important: the shopping centre and the airport. Quiet contemplation in the museum gallery is still possible of course – if you go early on Tuesday, or load the CD-ROM, thereby saving the travel costs and, in the case of the Victoria & Albert, the admission fee.' Thank you very much.

Charles Jencks: We turn now to Lucio Passarelli, who is a civil engineer and from the Academia Nazionale di San Luca and the Pontificia Academia del Pantheon in Rome. He is in charge of artistic monuments in the Vatican. It turns out that Lucio is one of those three brothers who designed a building that I illustrated in the first edition of *Post-Modern Architecture*, which was somewhat criticised in Britain for being 'schizoid' because it involved three different styles, three different parts. I was defending the building for this very set of contradictions. In another sense, therefore, Lucio is an appropriate person to be speaking about this contradictory subject.

Lucio Passarelli: Firstly I wish to try and answer two original questions posed to me by the Academy Forum: have art galleries and museums replaced religion in the role of cultural centre piece? I sincerely believe that the notable development of museum culture in this century very simply can be attributed to a significant rise in recreational time, sponsored by a reduction in working hours and, to a lesser degree, the presence of the new cultural trends and interests.

The relationship between the church and the museum is not incidental however; the church historically supporting artistic production has often been the vessel for the display of art, thus creating a tie between the tourist and art viewer and the faithful on the pilgrimage. We can also say that the work of art can provoke a sense of ascendance both in the creator and in the viewer; a sense that I think exists in each one of us.

Instead, the relationship between an original work of art and religion is even more fundamental. While the holy touch imparted by an original work of art cannot act as a substitute for religious experience, an act of faith is required in the presence of any original because it must be admitted that recognition of difference between an original and a copy is reserved to very few people. Incidentally, I look forward to the development of global data banks composed of both physical and virtual art reproduction in the coming years. The prospect of a universal museum enclosed in a single room is an exciting addition to a museum original.

We are now involved in the design phase of a collaborative project for support services at the Vatican Museum. The construction must be completed in time for jubilee of the year 2000. The situation at present in the Vatican Museum is that you enter it on the left from a single entrance and exit only from one point. The museum is composed of four sections – the Sistine Chapel, the sculpture museum, the painting gallery and the new museum – with only this particular entrance and exit and a small connecting porch.

The future design is in its early stages. In this, the old entrance will become the exit only, while the new entrance will be to the side. A multi-layered pre-museum will contain security, cloakroom, tickets, commercial services, a restaurant and so on. There will be only one point of control and a diagonal connection by pedestrian ramp, escalator and elevator for a height of about 20 metres. This connects with a multi-level post-museum and distribution service, where the upper level will provide access to the four levels of the museum. In short, we have the pre-museum with services, the distribution, the post-museum and the museum proper.

Paul Finch: Frans Haks, your idea for the Groninger Museum – working with four or five architects and designers – raises the whole question of contradictions and difference, and spectacular ones at that: the question of the title and the agenda of a museum today in the 1990s being a place of spectacular contradictions. Words that we heard very strongly put earlier by Derek and Guy, you will see handled in a very architectural way. Frans Haks.

Frans Haks: Thank you. First of all the Groninger Museum has several collections of archaeological and regional history, Eastern ceramics, old master paintings and contemporary art. When I was appointed rector in 1978 I concentrated on contemporary art. I thought that a very specific kind of building should be the product of the exceptional donation to the museum, which came

from a gas company. The point of departure was to have a pavilion built for each collection, designed by several architects; the main one being Alessandro Mendini. For example, the lower part of the pavilion on one side of the scheme is executed in brick by Michele de Lucchi and the upper, circular part, executed in aluminium by Philippe Starck. On the other side, the lower part of the pavilion is by Mendini and the upper part by Coop Himmelblau.

In the centre of the composition a tower houses general functions such as the entrance, the café and storage space. You go downstairs to access the various pavilions. In the corridor you can't see outside the building but you are aware of the water, which is more or less to the level of your hip. You then come to an oval room that leads to the historical pavilion by Michele de Lucchi. The idea was really to create different kinds of atmosphere in the general parts and in the pavilions.

Basically, the collection is split up into periods, each with its own pavilion in which the works of art or the historical objects are wholly integrated. Mendini and I agreed that in the rooms where art was exhibited we would not allow any daylight since it was too complicated to have this well-regulated and we preferred, according to the different atmosphere that we wanted to create, to have all kinds of spotlights and general lighting.

As soon as you recognise art as art, we think that the building can become more competitive. If you show contemporary art and the art is itself strange and difficult enough then you should have a calm and more serene background, exemplified by Mendini's section.

Paul Finch: It seems that you have built in a way that we heard about with the other museums, but it is more dramatised. I wonder if you feel as a former director, that the contradictions, the forces on the museum, as you were creating it, were such that you wanted to express them. But did they in the end take control of the museum?

Frans Haks: What we had in mind was to create another type of museum. Therefore we questioned every aspect of the nature of the museum and the design process; for example, we found that it was better not to use daylight. Also, natural architecture, in our opinion, does not exist – white rooms are not natural at all. So all these matters were discussed and it was not on purpose that contradictions emerged.

We wished to create a museum that would be considered very typical for the time; so, for example, no distinction was made between architecture and design. Mendini's experience working with other architects was related more to the field of furniture, but we felt that this could be extended to architecture. People often remark that a building is not architecture if it is not designed by an architect. They forget, I suppose, that the same kind of discussion evolved with railway stations in the past: that the work of engineers is not architecture.

To answer your question, the idea was not to create contradictions but to enlarge the concept of what a museum is. For example, the way in which the Disneyland pavilions attract one's attention for more than a day is much stronger than any museum I know. We therefore thought it very worthwhile to study the principles of Disneyland and assess the extent to which these could be applied. Also, if a warehouse has a better display than a museum, to 'borrow' this manner of display. Moreover, we made lists of everything that should be avoided.

To return to your question again, contradiction was not the

idea. Enlarging the concept of the museum was the idea. Originally, we planned to involve architects from different continents but this did not happen. In terms of the spectacular, well I can't speak for Mendini because he is as different as I am. It is of course a kind of spectacular thing, but that was not the main point. The objective was to create something that was very attractive and this, well this is to do with another kind of thing . . .

Robert Maxwell: It seems to me that this is a very clear example of a skilful presentation of the art in a building that is also art. While one would not want to say this is bad, at the same time one has a small worm of worry that everything today is becoming staged – everything is becoming a stage set. It is not only Disney that recreates the past for us in an easy and simple way, it is now serious museums that make entertainment for us so that their museum becomes an attraction on the tourist route. It seems to me that we are now competing for the attention of a public where the standards are provided by department stores, shopping malls and airports, and no longer by churches.

Frans Haks: Of course there is nothing wrong with churches, only their goal is wrong. An important factor is the way the building is used and the concentration is focused; for example, the use of steps towards the altar was something that we had considered not for the purpose of ascent but to use as a kind of stage. If you have one room with more than one piece to exhibit you are forced to direct – to stage – in one or another way. I don't think there is anything wrong with that. As the staging has always been there, and is always different, I think that the task is to try to progress a step further.

Paul Finch: I wonder if I could make an observation and perhaps bring in Hans Hollein. From the projects we have seen this afternoon there is this sense that the places which display the originals, the authentic, seem to want to be more and more rooted in archaeology. We saw it very clearly in the submerging of the Groninger Museum and in the underground section of Passarelli's scheme for the Vatican.

I wonder if this is a response to the fact that no one has to go there any more to see the things which they can perhaps watch on television, buy a CD-ROM or get a catalogue. Perhaps this sort of physical manifestation of the permanent is actually an attempt to provide some sort of authentic building, some sort of original deeply-rooted thing which responds to those contents in a completely different way to the behaviour of the people looking at the stuff inside the space.

Hans Hollein: I think that we are at the stage where, as has been done in the Groninger Museum, there are different ways to approach a work of art. One of these, which wasn't mentioned during the time I was here, is the question of aura which is very important in relation to authenticity.

In terms of the elimination of hierarchy, seen in the scheme for the Groninger Museum, I think this is basically right, but I don't know if it works everywhere. Certain hierarchies have an advantage in their structure and can help you to have access to works of art as you gradually ascend. I don't think you can equalise any exhibit. I am not agreeing with the idea of staging. My perception of the Groninger Museum is, in a way, that the content is extremely traditional and there is very little vision concerning the art of the future, in terms of media and video.

Frans Haks: I don't agree that the collection does not cater for the future, but one could say that it is not as strong as the building. However, I do think that if you have the opportunity to build a museum it should be as good as is possible, and of this time. Also, the care you take over the presentation should be the optimum, even if the collection is perhaps not the best.

Paul Finch: Peter Cook would you like to make a comment on what you've heard?

Peter Cook: Yes. I think that the museum business – not talking so much about art galleries but museums – has, as many believe, to do with the setting of an aura. I know from my childhood, which was mostly spent in British cities of Roman origin, that the impression given to you was that you were on the site of, or in the presence of, the ghost of Rome, or of Roman Britain. It is likely that several layers exist: for example, the actual thing, the near presence of the actual thing, the thing that looks like the actual thing, the thing that might look like the actual thing and the thing that does not attempt to look like the actual thing.

So there is an element of tease that is played between the objects. To what extent do you as an organiser of phenomena play a series of games with it, whether the series of games is theatrical or not? I don't know the answer, I merely put forth a little of the problem.

I visited the Groninger Museum with 60 art students – a mixed bag from London, Vienna and Frankfurt – some with very in-built responses, shall we say, to some of the art that was presented. The Groninger collection rather fell on its face from time to time, while at other times it was brilliant. We felt that most of the designers – not just Coop Himmelblau but the other designers as well – were thinking on their feet and the general reaction was more positive, perhaps because we spend all our time in these art/architectural contrivances and we rather enjoy seeing a building which has a sort of richness of risk.

In a sense, one enjoys buildings where there is this knife edge sometimes between kitsch and brilliance. When you walk into the Himmelblau part of the Groninger Museum it sounds like a ship. I was actually taking a video and what really comes across when playing it back is the sound of being in a ship's hull, of seeing the water reflected and the risk of going over that triangular patterned glass.

OK, we can call this show business, and I must admit that when we were there, no exhibition was showing. We had to imagine what it might be like so we were really in the dodgy position of seeing the building raw. But I thought that it worked tremendously well in that old kind of palace tradition of moving from chamber to chamber to chamber; each bit of it different. The part dealing with ancient objects was extremely well-lit and I was probably more interested in looking at the lighting than the enclosures, which is perhaps a compliment to the enclosures.

I think that all of these things are related and I don't think it is particularly to do with the present period. I suspect that were we talking about this at the point of the invention of electricity, or the invention of the film slide, there would have been parallel conversations.

From the floor: It seems to me that quite a lot of the discussion this afternoon revolves around the rather more 19th-century notion of a museum. I am reminded of an essay by Walter Benjamin in the 1930s relating to art and mechanical reproduction in which he envisaged the increased erosion of an aura this century. I think it is very fitting that we have ended by looking at the Groninger Museum. To me it represents the only critical piece of architecture that we've seen today, in that it raises important questions about the context, about what is the done thing, what is the proper way of seeing art in all its seriousness – beyond a sense of the history of art, or history of 20th-century Western culture.

You get a historiographical understanding of what it is to examine art at this moment in the 20th century, which is done without recourse to CD-ROM, without recourse to technology and yet begs all those questions. It is very interesting today that this has been the one thing that has agitated – if you don't mind me saying so – a lot of grey men in suits.

Paul Finch: There seems to be another reason why one can say that the Groninger Museum is the most critical piece of architecture we have seen and that is that it is explicitly about the rebirth of the visitor as the performer. There is a move towards interaction, and I don't just mean with interactive technology, although that is obviously part of it. You go to a museum as a performance, as a right, rather than as some sort of awestruck little piece of social detritus who is obviously there only to be educated in the ways of the moving classes.

Geoffrey Broadbent: I am very intrigued by the way that the idea of performance has emerged, because the whole point of the stage set is to enhance the play so that we can understand much more about it and certainly that is true in the Groninger Museum. In every place I went to the art was enhanced: the ceramics looked more ceramic-like than any ceramics I have seen anywhere before. That was true of the Old Masters and the recent paintings. The stage-set quality actually makes the art show through much better.

Michael Brawne: Could I ask why there should not be some awe when going to a museum. Might we not actually go to museums because we are in awe of something that is different to that of everyday life? I mean, earlier on we had an analogy that museums were the substitute for churches, and certainly churches were built in order to create this sense of awe and were popular exactly because they did that. So maybe museums are different and should be deliberately different from the everyday in order to provide another kind of experience. If every experience is at the level of the most ordinary, no experience has any value.

Jeremy Melvin: I don't think we were defending the idea of awe Michael. But I would like to ask Mr Passarelli about the pre-museum and the post-museum in terms of the way in which contradictory things are asked of the museum today: that is to say, there is a space before you even reach the museum which sells art objects, books . . . whatever, which has three storeys, for example in the Vatican. So after you have been to the space and have had a three-second experience of looking at the Sistine Ceiling, you come back and you probably have a post-experience where you re-buy the book for the second time. But is it not the case that we have an extended experience now, that the experience has been divided into three parts: the pre-experience, the experience and the post-experience. Is that right?

Lucio Passarelli: I think that we must bring to a real level the emphasis that we put on the commercial part of the museum,

which I don't think will be a very successful economic activity despite the increased popular demand. One of the many problems posed now by the museum is how to put a commercial section in an environment like the Vatican Palace; for me the most important problem posed by the museum.

Paul Finch: On that note I am going to draw things to a close. I think that this is an appropriate moment actually, because the dilemmas posed by the combination of what are apparently conflicting or contradictory activities that are taking place in these cultural containers is something which architects are grappling with, and I feel that we are only scratching at the surface. One only has to think about the impact of the cinema on museums and galleries and essentially until very recently it was absolute zero and there still isn't very much done – the nearest thing to this is a museum about photography and film where it has to be engaged because that is the nature of the programme.

This afternoon we have wondered about how you put the awe into aura and whether creating an aura is what museums are about, or perhaps at least creating an atmosphere. We have looked at the notion of the authentic, and of course in London authentic has itself become a strange word – I mean, one says authentic but not in a Tate Gallery sense, and I suppose that we are all having to become accustomed to the notion of the authentic fake.

The idea of the difference between sculpture and architecture being plumbing I felt provided an undercurrent to some of the discussions this afternoon, especially in respect of the distinction that was made earlier between the two types of museum: the museum which is in essence a display case – perhaps like the Royal Armouries Museum, which clearly sets out to provide its public with the best possible experience of its contents – and then later on with the notion proposed by the Groninger Museum: that of the museum as art object; a building which one might go to even if there is no display inside it, and which validates itself in its own right.

I was very interested in the comment made by Frans Haks in relation to the Groninger Museum about what one could or could not learn from Disney. On a previous occasion at an Academy Forum event we went into this in some detail and I think it is fascinating to hear that Haks went there explicitly to see how they staged things, how they used them and of course what to avoid. And this phrase 'we stole as much as we could and noted what to avoid' seems to me an admirable way to approach any experience involving Disney itself.

Then of course we had Robert Maxwell's point, that everything these days is becoming staged. I suppose that if one regards that as sinister one can at least take comfort in the fact that it has become an option as to whether one visits this proliferation of museums and galleries.

More people are visiting them. Whether or not that is a temporary phenomenon, I think, is partly going to be up to the museums and galleries themselves as they think and decide about whether the way they want to display their collections is via the Internet, via electronic means, which are not to do with the rootedness or the design of their own building, but are to do with collections that they own.

I would like to thank Academy Group again for sponsoring this occasion, and to thank MaryAnne Stevens and the Royal Academy once again for their hospitality and for allowing us to hold the event in one of London's greatest stage-sets.

THE MUSEUM AS A MIRROR OF SOCIETY
CLARE MELHUISH

In May and June of this year, a number of museums and galleries across London collaborated in putting on a series of exhibitions under the overall title *Collected*. The theme encompassed a self-critical look at the role of museums and why we have them, which drew on anthropological and psychoanalytical theory. The intention was to highlight the way in which societies accumulate, classify and present material objects, creating patterns of practice that reveal innate values and ideals, presented as public culture. Thus the gathering, selection and organisation of material objects becomes a system through which society constructs a particular public image of itself.

The history of collecting is very long, but it was in Renaissance Italy that the idea of the museum as a modern institution was born. In the 19th century the museum really became established as the accepted site of collecting, and most of the great national collections of Europe are housed in buildings constructed at this time. Three of the *Collected* sites fell into this category: the Hunterian Museum at the Royal College of Surgeons in Lincoln's Inn Fields, the British Museum, and the Wallace Collection (a private mansion bequeathed to the state). The less conventional nature of the other sites – the Photographers' Gallery, two major department stores, Selfridges and Habitat, and a private residence – drew attention to the way that traditional ideas about museums and collections have changed in this century, particularly since the Second World War.

The unique role of the state-run museum to express a society's image of itself has been questioned, allowing multiple new images, based on alternative value systems, to be presented through different types of collections on alternative sites. To a very large extent this process has opened up a democratisation of public culture which can be seen as part of the process of a perceived 'fragmentation' of society. In other words, the unified, homogeneous image of society sustained by the establishment through its channels of influence and propagation has been blown away to reveal the true variety of values and aspirations that lay behind it, now hugely increased by the rise of multiculturalism in all the great metropolitan centres of the world.

The dramatic rise of the museum in 19th-century Europe (from fewer than 12 in 1800, to nearly 60 by 1850, and at least 240 by 1887) was closely allied to industrialisation. As the pace of social change increased, so too did an anxiety to gather up and conserve artefacts from the past which provided some point of moral reference for society, and a sense of continuity. At the same time, the new collections served to illustrate and reinforce the ideology of linear progress which underpinned and sustained the whole Industrial Revolution. The collection and presentation of pieces of material culture provided public evidence of the ever-advancing progress of human rationale and man's control over his environment, and the increasing sophistication of society. It also served to validate the capitalist, material-wealth-based foundations of social status, and to promote a sense of national identity and solidity which was of prime political importance during an era when the nation-states of Europe were developing an increasing self-awareness and confrontational attitude to each other which was eventually to erupt in the First World War.

These roots are explored by the anthropologist Susan Pearce in her cultural study on museums and their contents. She explains that the 19th-century museum was designed very much as a piece of ceremonial architecture in which the idea of the sacred was translated into secular and national or civic terms and linked with a conviction in progress:

> The building, its iconography, its gallery layout and its sequence of collections together provide what Victor Turner called a 'script' or 'doing code' to be performed by individuals, alone or in groups. The walk around the galleries has been paced out by those before us, and anticipated emotions are aroused by the deliberate rhythms of case and structure: we emerge tired (ritual is always demanding), sometimes exalted, always with a feeling of piety, of duty satisfactorily performed.[1]

This notion of the museum as essentially playing the function of temple of the Muses generated an overwhelming preference for the use of the Neoclassical and Greek Revival styles in museum design across Europe. However, these ideas were to be dramatically altered in the 20th century, which Pearce attributes to a 'growing romantic attachment to local communities and cultures', fast disappearing under the impact of industrialisation and urbanisation. The traditional inward focus of museums on their collections began to shift in favour of a more outward-going attitude towards communities.

Simultaneously, as Stephen Weil discusses, the rise of the media meant that the museum became less important as a medium for the dissemination of information: the media serves that purpose as least as effectively as exhibits, and 'the museum's voice is no longer seen as transcendent'.[2] Furthermore, society as a whole has become more aware of the way that factual information is shaped and presented by a larger social order and its values, and of the role that the museum might play in that process. An increasing unhappiness has developed about the ease with which the museum can be used as an ideological tool of the state. These changes in social attitudes have opened up a wide-ranging debate about the role, function and design of the museum and, simultaneously, a huge increase in the number of museums, of which Europe now boasts around 13,500, with 5,000 of those in Britain alone, and the rest of the world some 12,000.

Anthropologists have defined a classic distinction between the role of museum as Temple, prevalent in the 19th century, and the role of museum as Forum – much more common today, at least as an ideal, though whether this is so in practice or not is debatable. The recasting of the status and iconography of the museum has led directly to major changes in the architecture and organisation of museum buildings, such that the 'ritualistic' quality of the 19th-century museum layout and intended experience described by

Susan Pearce has been challenged. As Forum, the contemporary museum is supposed to offer what anthropologists Efrat Ben-Ze'ev and Eyal Ben-Ari have described, in an article on the Tourjeman Post Museum in Jerusalem, as 'a place of confrontation, experimentation and debate'.[3] That is, a place of encounter and interrelationship between the visitors themselves, not simply between the visitors and the collections. Stephen Weil casts the visitor as 'collaborator', and the role of the Forum-museum as one of 'stimulation and empowerment'.[4]

In order to achieve these ideals, museums all over the world have embraced a new architectural order based on an idea of accessibility and legibility which was fundamentally validated by the 1969 study, *The Love of Art*, by the French anthropologists Pierre Bourdieu and Alain Darbel.[5] In this book (based on extensive research carried out through subjecting the visiting public of museums in France, Spain, Greece, Holland, Italy and Poland to questionnaires, sampling, surveys and 'semi-directed' interviews) Bourdieu demonstrated that access to cultural works was 'the privilege of the cultivated class', and challenged its legitimation. On the basis of his evidence, he argued that:

> Those who did not receive the instruments which imply familiarity with art from their family or from their schooling are condemned to a perception of a work of art which takes its categories from the experience of everyday life and which results in the basic recognition of the object depicted . . .
>
> Totally reliant on the museum and the aids it provides, they ['uncultivated' visitors] are particularly out of their depth in museums which deliberately address themselves to the cultivated public. 77 per cent . . . would like the help of a guide or a friend, 67 per cent would like the visit to be signposted with arrows, and 89 per cent would like the works to be supplemented by explanatory panels.

Bourdieu points out that:

> arrows, notices, guidebooks, guides or receptionists would not really make up for a lack of education, but they would proclaim, simply by existing, the right to be uninformed, the right to be there and uninformed, and the right of uninformed people to be there: they would help to minimise the apparent inaccessibility of the works and of the visitors' feeling of unworthiness . . .

Bourdieu overtly challenged the presumption of cultural superiority by those who 'think that ritual asceticism and Cistercian starkness are . . . the only means of attaining communion with a work of art', and research of this nature underpinned dramatic changes in the way that museums began to present themselves, both in terms of exhibition design and the presentation of collections, and in the provision of back-up facilities – educational, social, and commercial. Lecture theatres, restaurants, shops became essential components in the museum complex, while exhibition spaces were expected to provide increasing flexibility. The museum was to be transformed from civic monument to community building, and the iconographic trappings of the Temple discarded in favour of secular garb inspired by indigenous reference.

George F MacDonald, director of the Canadian Museum of Civilisation (CMC), designed by Douglas Cardinal in 1989, describes the modern museum as an 'information institution', stressing the way that the development of 'non-material resource' collections – such as oral histories, photography, re-enactments – has changed the nature of the traditional museum.[6] He defines the three fundamental needs of visitors as 'intellectual, sacred, and social': to know and understand, to link with one's ancestral past and undertake rites of passage conferring social status (the museum as pilgrimage site), and to 'be seen' and socialise.

While this suggests on the one hand an enhancement of the 'ritualistic qualities of some experiences', it has also prompted an emphasis on education and entertainment inspired by 'careful study of Disney theme parks early in the building project for CMC'. Lobbies, lounges, theatres, and restaurants play a crucial role in the social functioning of the museum, while shops are important providers of 'take-away materials' intended to fuel a new interest and encourage further investigation, and professional actors are employed to recreate historic events.

Indeed, CMC has been described by critics as 'Disney in the North', but MacDonald emphasises that although theme parks have high presentation standards which he believes worthy of emulation, information content standards are low. This would be unacceptable at the museum. He is motivated in his presentation of CMC by the understanding that multicultural societies, such as Canada's, require very different things of the museum institution from what it has traditionally offered.

CMC is perhaps an extreme example of the museum reinterpreted as Forum. By contrast, the Groninger Museum in The Netherlands, designed by Alessandro Mendini in 1994, is inspired by a rather different vision – the design developed out of the concept of 'artistic architecture', with a 'symmetrical, ancient, sharply iconic and ritual plan'. The aim was to achieve an 'object-phenomenon' with a high narrative complexity:

> There is no interruption between the building's self-museumisation and a living museumisation of the works exhibited in it. Thus the building will in itself be a system of museum works, while the exhibits integrate with and interpenetrate the architecture that receives and expresses them.

If one is to believe Bourdieu's research, much of this would pass over the heads of the 'uncultivated' visitor, and Mendini's vision seems directed more at a self-aware, artistically and architecturally cultivated audience, even though he claims that the building represents the three ideals of 'the cosmos intended as an aesthetic totality, of artistic creativity as the prerogative of all men, and of asserting itself as an anti-monument, as a message against cultural terrorism'.

In France, which has encouraged a prolific wave of museum building over the last couple of decades, there is a fascinating contrast between projects such as the Pompidou Centre, the Louvre pyramid, or the Nîmes Mediathèque. The Pompidou, constructed in the 1970s, has, as is well-known, outstripped its intended popular appeal so far that the building itself has been unable to stand such intense use, and less than 20 years on requires major refurbishment. The Pompidou epitomised new ideas about museum culture in the 1970s, designed as a warehouse-like, explicitly functional building, in which art was to be displayed as a commodity rather than as a revered object. The wide piazza outside was designed to play an overtly social role, so that the street-life which developed outside and in front of the 'museum' became almost more important than its contents. This was the new society of post-1968, dominated by youthful ideals of informality and art for all. The implications of the museum spread even beyond the building to touch the fabric of the city itself, since a large chunk of the historic centre of Paris had to be demolished to make way for the new structure.

By contrast, the Louvre pyramid (commissioned essentially because the Louvre was upset at the way in which the Pompidou had overtaken its attendance figures) is a formalist project driven by political intent of a somewhat different nature. Central to President Mitterrand's programme of *Grands Projets*, designed to enhance the political prestige of Paris as well as to ensure that his own legacy as president would not be easily forgotten, the glass pyramid designed by IM Pei is usually described as a failure in terms of its programme, yet it has achieved an undoubted iconic status. It was designed to provide a new entrance to the museum, leading into an expanse of new underground accommodation including a shopping arcade, cafés and car-parking. However the entrance, via escalators underneath the glass pyramid, proved to be far too constricted for the numbers of visitors flocking to see the collections – and the new building itself.

The simple, easily recognisable geometry of the Louvre pyramid was typical of the *Grands Projets*, and reflected Mitterrand's personal architectural preference. The rationalism of pure form was intended as a mirror of an ordered society governed by enlightenment principles; the transparency of the building also typified a strong tendency in French public architecture towards the use of glass, symbolising the transparency of democracy. Following Mitterrand's lead, local mayors all over the country commissioned 'lightweight' glass buildings which would convey a different message from the ponderous masonry constructions of the past. Amongst these was the Nîmes Mediathèque and Centre for Contemporary Art by Norman Foster, on the site, significantly, of the old Neoclassical theatre damaged by fire in 1951.

The 'mediathèque', or information centre, is a specifically French concept which creates an image of France at the forefront of information technology: a continuation of the tradition of the Minitel, a basic form of computer which all French people had in their homes alongside the telephone from the 1970s onwards, to provide them with access to information sources, such as ticket bureaux. Ironically, the very presence of a mediathèque within a contemporary art gallery serves to throw into question the significance of the objects themselves. Nevertheless, the Nîmes building is seen as providing a shiny new symbol of French political and cultural values, while at the same time sticking to a more or less Beaux-Arts, symmetrical form of internal organisation which reinforces the classic symbolism of the ordered society. Views out over the square confirm the building's role in the traditional urban configuration of the city. Thus, despite the emphasis on dissemination of information and interaction with the public, the Mediathèque presents an image which is still very

closely allied with the Temple concept which inspired museum architecture and organisation in the past.

In sensitive political situations, the museum, its organisation and iconography is fully exposed as an intense political arena. In the case of the Tourjeman Post Museum, as in many, the creation of the museum was 'part of a decades long link between nation building and the establishment of museums in modern Israel'.[7] The renewal programme, initiated amidst the euphoria which followed the peace process of the early 1990s, was intended to transform the museum, which had been devoted to Israeli heroism, into a museum of co-existence: a forum in which the narratives of the Israelis and the Palestinians could be set out side by side in a context of discussion and debate.

One idea was to explore ways of presenting Jerusalem as a holy city, making it unique among other divided cities. Other proposals included showing images of different areas, activities and identities in the city, to build up a picture of a 'mosaic of diverse ingredients', a harmonious multiculturalism, which omitted any sense of conflict. However dissenting voices, such as that of a Palestinian newspaper editor, who insisted that the museum should portray the war of 1967 from the Palestinian perspective, exposed the underlying idea of Israeli paternalism. 'A representative of a formal political Palestinian institution considered cooperating with the museum, but clarified from the beginning that her institution demanded that the Palestinians present themselves without the mediation of the museum as an Israeli institution', report the authors of the study.

The building itself was designed by an Arab architect, Andoni Baramki, a Christian Palestinian who studied in Greece and incorporated indigenous Palestinian elements of Jerusalemite stone with Greek pillars in his design. It is located at the edge of the Jewish part of the city and so remains to an extent part of the Jewish frontier. According to traditional Israeli museum practice, visitors are given an orientation to the site's narrative before entering it. In this case, they are advised to begin their tour on the roof, offering a panoramic view in which, however, Israeli visitors are able to identify only a very few of the surrounding places. Amongst these is Mount Scopus in the north, a former Israeli army enclave within Arab territory.

The external restoration of the building has been based on its reconstruction as an army post: 'by walking on the roof and within the building itself, visitors are made to feel like soldiers peering out into the surroundings.' Hence the museum's military connections, from an Israeli point of view, are firmly emphasised, contradicting the message of peace and co-existence and the potential role of the museum as Forum.

Interestingly enough, as the authors point out, the Palestinians themselves, 'have not, as yet, begun to use on a large scale such cultural institutions to disseminate their collective narrative'. Correspondingly, as George MacDonald indicates, there is a trend in some 'developing' countries to use the name 'cultural centre', suggesting a concept of ownership by a community or communities, as an alternative to the whole concept of the museum and its connotations of power, hierarchy, and ritual.

In Britain, a whole new generation of 'arts buildings' is being spawned by the Lottery, few of which will be described as museums. The sudden availability of funding has prompted a rash of projects which attempt to redefine the parameters of design of such buildings, such that they reflect public expectations more accurately than their historic counterparts are now able to do. Amongst these is the new Walsall Art Gallery, the

Groninger museum, Groningen, The Netherlands, Alessandro and Francesco Mendini, Michele de Lucchi, Philippe Starck, Coop Himmelblau

building of which starts this summer. This institution houses the world-class Kathleen Garman Collection, but was also one of the first to invite local communities to use the museum as an arena in which to show their own collections to each other. The construction of the new building is regarded as an essential element in the regeneration of the town as a whole. Significantly, questionnaires sent out to the local community to gauge the level of its approval for the project were nearly all returned with an affirmative response to the question, did the town need a new art gallery? – even though most of those who responded in the affirmative also stated that they would probably never visit it themselves.

These factors are reflected in a design by Caruso St John which presents the art gallery as a tall landmark, visible across the town above the skyline of the surrounding shopping centre; yet which is also described, in domestic terms, as a 'big house', and places heavy emphasis on educational areas for children

and adults, social areas including a café and restaurant, and external public, civic space around the building.

The unusual aspect of the Lottery-funded buildings in Britain is that they are all required to have majority public approval as a condition of funding. This implies a radical potential rethinking of the traditional museum as a mirror of a society's ideals and aspirations, as channelled through the power structures and particular social make-up of the establishment. The necessity of public consensus suggests the formalisation of a process by which the content and presentation of cultural institutions is opened up for discussion and decision-making by a much wider sector of society than formerly, when the reigns of control were held very firmly by the state or by private patrons who walked in circles close to the sources of political power. The implications of this for the architecture of the museum interpreted afresh, are complex and will gradually unfold over the next few years.

Notes

1 Susan M Pearce, *Museums, Objects and Collections: a Cultural Study*, Leicester University Press, 1992.

2 Stephen E Weil, *Rethinking the Museum and other Meditations*, Smithsonian Institute, 1990.

3 Efrat Ben-Ze'ev and Eyal Ben-Ari, 'Imposing Politics: failed attempts at creating a museum of "co-existence" in Jerusalem', *Anthropology Today*, Vol 12, No 6, December 1996.

4 Ibid.

5 Pierre Bourdieu and Alain Darbel, *The Love of Art*, English translation, Polity Press, 1991; original French version, *L'Amour de l'art: les musées d'art européens et leur public*, Les Editions de Minuit, 1969.

6 George F MacDonald, 'Change and Challenge', in *Museums and Communities: the politics of public culture*, Ivan Karp (ed), Smithsonian Institute, 1992.

7 Efrat Ben-Ze'ev and Eyal Ben-Ari, op cit.

26

GÜNTER ZAMP KELP

THE NEANDERTHAL MUSEUM
Mettmann, Germany

Myth, site and time spiral

A museum for the history of human evolution must live up to both the myth of the Neanderthal as a place, and to the contents presented inside the museum. In the proposed design, superimposing the idea of place with the uniqueness of the exhibited subject matter and the building itself creates an unmistakable scenario. The central theme of the building is a spiral-shaped ramp which provides access to the different exhibition areas and defines the building's character. The loop-like ramp spiral, as synonym for eternity, transforms the building into a spatial parable of the evolution of humankind, which is, after all, part of eternity.[1]

I was still a schoolboy when I first heard of the Neanderthal man and his significance in the history of human evolution. Without knowing about the place that gave the historic bone discovery its name, pictures of primitive landscapes appeared in my mind, full of forests and horsetail vegetation, and populated by a variety of archaic beasts, and primitive humans wrapped in fur.

I only discovered once I had followed the name of the valley to gain a better sense of the place that today the area around the Neanderthal constitutes a recreational area for the towns of Mettmann, Düsseldorf and Wuppertal. One's first impression is dominated by the normality of a green valley, traversed by a water course. However, when reading about the history of the place, descriptions emerge of the destruction of a remarkable landscape through the exploitation of limestone. Not much of the one time 'natural wonder' remains.

The valley has paid for its evolutionary fame with the loss of the landscape's uniqueness. Without the exploitation of limestone, however, the bones of the Neanderthal man may never have surfaced. Today the quarry is inactive and the valley has been declared a landscape conservation area. Along the road connecting Düsseldorf to Mettmann there are three remarkable objects of architectural note.

The first of these is a square-plan, glass tower in the vicinity of a glassworks. The second is a highway bridge that spans the valley's spacious end and derives its character from the monumental substructure supporting the roadway above. The third curiosity is situated on one of the upper rims around the valley's centre: a silo compound painted white, with the aura of an acropolis.

Derive a meaning from this series of constructed oddities if you like; in any case, the construction of the Neanderthal Museum represents a further element along the road between Mettmann and Düsseldorf. The form and function of the Neanderthal Museum are not in keeping with the existing architecture in the valley. Only the educational section, as one part of the building complex, relates in scale to the context. It is located on the site of a stone house that had to be removed due to disrepair, and largely takes on its size and proportions.

Within the new ensemble, the nature of the exhibition building as a 'construction' stands out, particularly when set against the normality of the valley's buildings and landscape.

The spiral shape of the exhibition building can be read on its facade. The building's shell is formed from a series of glass profiles, made up of two C-shaped elements each, and with the measurements of 4.0 x 0.5 x 0.1 metres. An aluminium structure connects the row of glass volumes on the facade to the building's bearing walls behind.

The spatial depth of the outer surfaces of the exhibition building contrasts with the fair-faced concrete surfaces inside. The cave-like quality created internally is evocative of the valley's long-gone atmosphere. The juxtaposition of the external appearance and cave-like interior corresponds to the museum's function as a medium between the past and the future of human evolution.

The shape of the spiral gives the impression of a space winding itself out of the earth towards the future evolution of human existence. This spatial spiral describes simultaneously our society's history and perspectives, as well as the relation between space and time. In this way, it corresponds to an understanding of locality similar to that of Marcel Proust: that places exist only in time, never in reality; that they are constantly changing, dissolving, melting and only in our memory do they stay what they then (at a given point in time) once were.[2]

Notes
1 Excerpt from the explanatory text of the competition entry.
2 Quoted in Klaus Mann, *Child of our Time*.

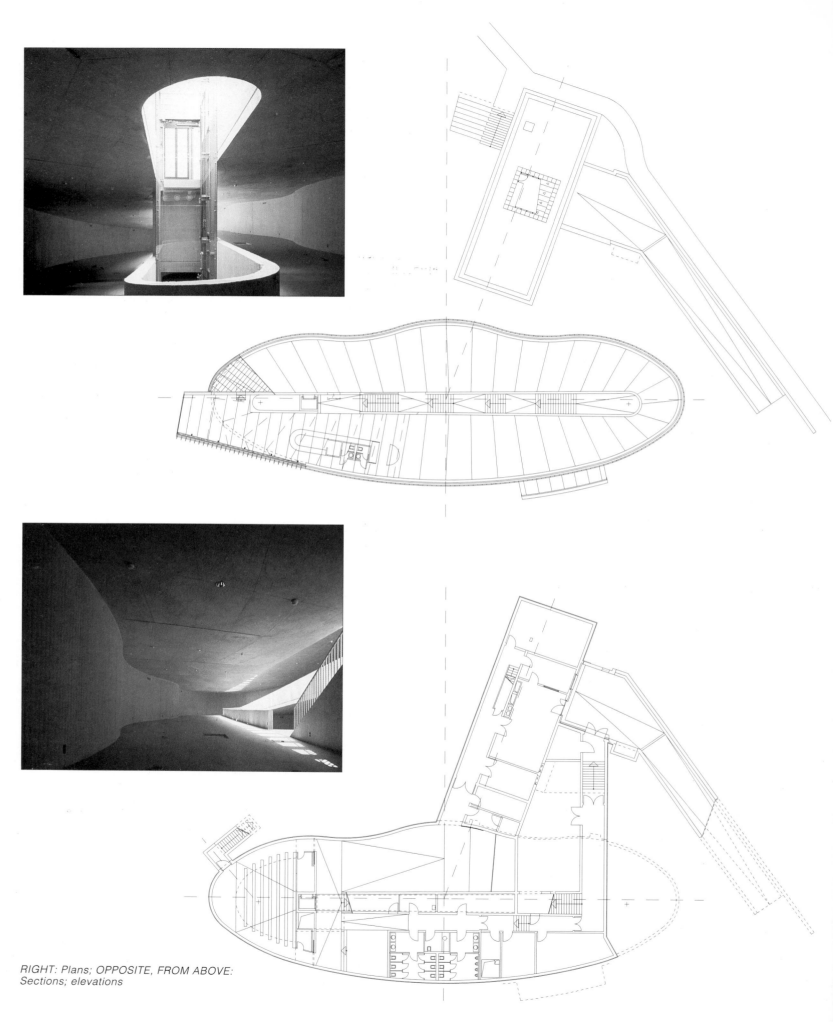

*RIGHT: Plans; OPPOSITE, FROM ABOVE:
Sections; elevations*

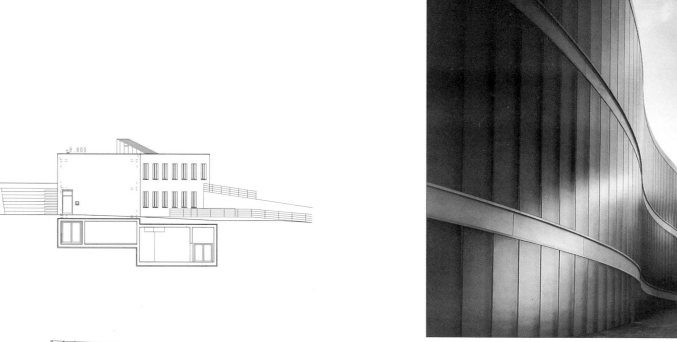

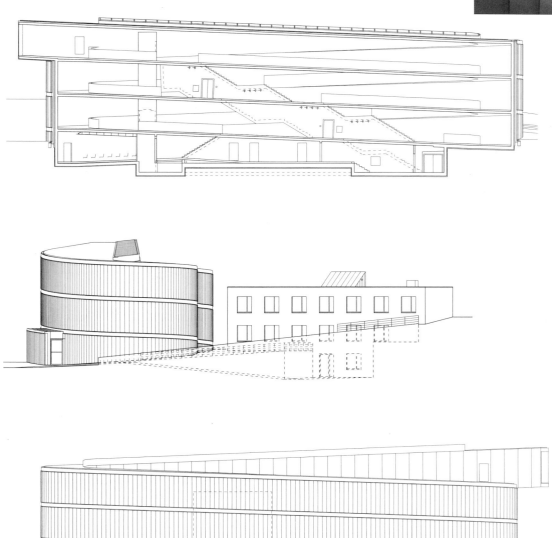

GEORG SCHÄFER MUSEUM
Schweinfurt, Germany

An important formal and organisational element regarding the presentation of the collection in the museum is the concept of the frame as a medium that intervenes between two-dimensional images and their surroundings. The frame of each painting (of which there are almost 300) separates it from and places it in relation to its background.

In this project, the frame becomes the theme for the museum building. The construction principle consists of space-forming frames which are installed one after another. This brings about the required span of 2 x 17 metres, using an existing subterranean garage as a base.

The museum, as a container for the paintings and drawings of the collection, becomes a space for storage and presentation as well as a space of identity relating to the urban neighbourhood.

As the frames of the exposed images mediate between pictures, contents and surroundings, so the components of the building are media between inner and outer space. In this way, the profile of the building conveys the function and contents of the museum to the surrounding urban area. A synthesis of concept and form is created by the 13 frames of the building and the framed art pieces inside the exhibition space.

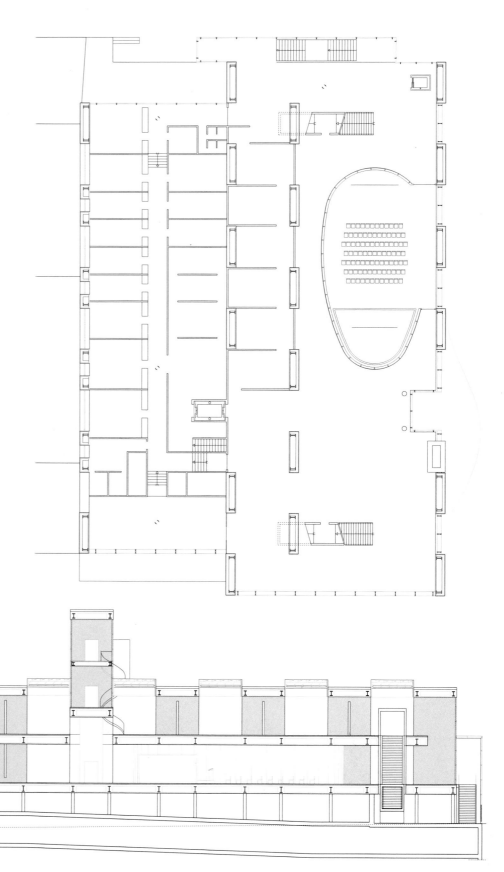

ABOVE: Plan; RIGHT: Section

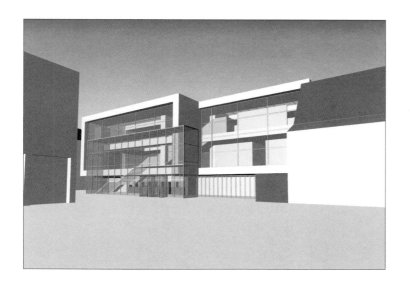

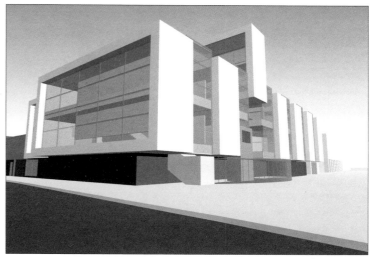

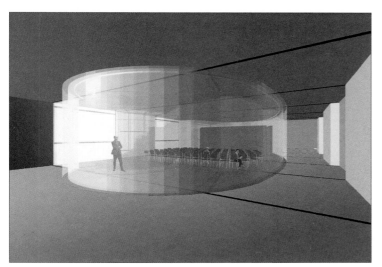

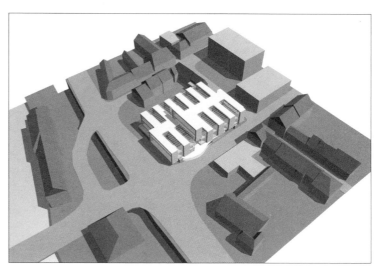

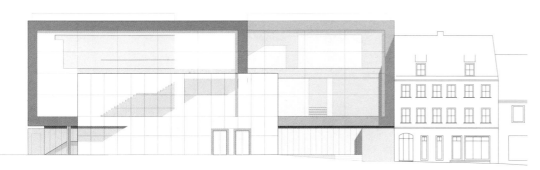

ABOVE: Computer-generated perspectives;
LEFT: Section

RAUTENSTRAUCH JOEST MUSEUM
Cologne

This project illustrates a constellation of ancillary buildings which relate to the scale of the neighbourhood, and an architectonic dominant that gives significance to the whole situation by its dimension and appearance. The oval form of its outer skin consists of 14 panels which are arranged in a manner that is reminiscent of archaic constructions like Stonehenge.

The cone-like form is positioned upside down in the city surface and is perceived as a metaphor for permanent world-population. The dynamic space between the outer skin and the inner exhibition building provides an area for panoramic scenes concerning ethnological configurations.

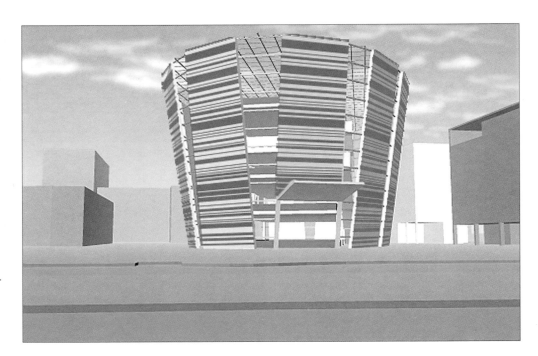

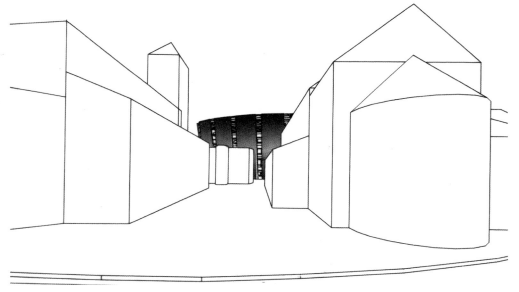

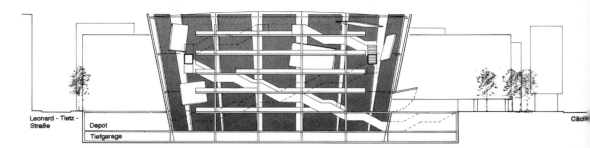

ABOVE AND CENTRE: Computer-generated perspectives; RIGHT: Sections

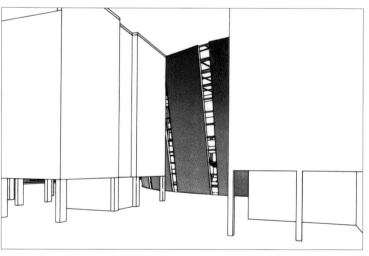

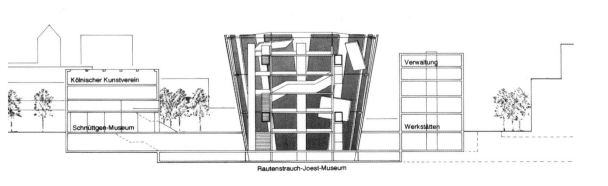

Kölnischer Kunstverein

Verwaltung

Schnüttgen-Museum

Werkstätten

Rautenstrauch-Joest-Museum

FRANS HAKS

GRONINGER MUSEUM
Groningen, The Netherlands

On the occasion of its 25th anniversary in 1987, Dutch Gas (*Gasunie*) donated 25 million guilders (£9 million) to build a new museum. As this was by far the biggest donation ever in The Netherlands for a cultural purpose by a commercial company, I felt obliged to come up with a concept for the new building which matched that exceptional gift

Rather than continue the historical tradition from Karl Friedrich von Schinkel in Berlin, to James Stirling in Stuttgart or Aldo Rossi in Maastricht, I preferred a more ambitious solution, like the Guggenheim Museum in New York or the Centre Pompidou in Paris. These museums initially received negative criticism but have proved to be of historical importance, becoming touristic attractions equal to that of the Eiffel Tower in Paris.

However, in seeking to reinvent the museological wheel, I discovered that it was not possible merely to follow the example set by one or more famous museums. Looking for inspiration in other fields I turned to literature, music and entertainment.

Johann Wolfgang von Goethe, in his conversations with Johann Peter Eckermann, asserted that if you concentrate on the colour green for a while, your eye automatically produces the complementary colour red in after-images. He based his colour theory on this observation and commented to Eckermann that man's need for variety was evident in every field of daily life. This need was so intense that the eye, the most sensitive human organ, would not even allow for the monotony of a long confrontation with one

colour: the eye becomes so irritated that it produces, itself, the contrasting colour.

Goethe wondered whether the need for variety, which is present in all other fields of human life, was responsible for Shakespeare weaving comical scenes into his tragedies. He felt that more pleasure could be gained from a musical composition which had a greater variety of modes. I admire the Italian composer Giuseppe Verdi for the way in which his operas succeed in holding one's attention for two hours or more. In a letter dated 1 January 1853, Verdi explained that he was always in search of new, diverse librettos. A few months later he explained that he was enamoured with the script for *Rigoletto* because it offered strong situations, diversity, vividness and pathos.

In connection with the première of

Bird's eye perspective of realised conception

Alessandro and Francesco Mendini, Central Building staircase

Macbeth in Paris, Verdi commented in a letter that the first Lady Macbeth, La Tadolini, was a beautiful and attractive woman but that she should be ugly and malicious. Although Tadolini's voice was beautiful, clear, and strong, a rough and strangled sound should be produced.

Thus, from Goethe and Verdi I learnt about the potential of contrasting sequences; from light to dark, from comedy to tragedy, from joy to sadness, or from beauty to ugliness. This gave me more confidence to explore a new type of museum building and more awareness of the variety that exists in other fields.

Even Disneyland, which specialises in entertainment for huge audiences, has based its philosophy on the laws of Goethe and Verdi: every kind of amusement is housed in an individual pavilion which is designed to function as a skin around a specific kind of pleasure.

These examples from quite different areas contrast with recent museum architecture. Many new museums are constructed with a minimum of materials and the spaces, regardless of their individual function, are pervaded by a universal atmosphere.

The creators of these museums evidently assume that it is possible to experience the delight of sublime art in a torturously dull or hostile environment. The 'guards' are dressed accordingly in military-style uniforms with the effect that the visitors are perceived as potential criminals. There are no uniforms in Disneyland but well-dressed, attractive and cordial people who offer help as soon as they assume you need it.

From these apparently insignificant observations of Disneyland and 'Museumland', evolved the basic concept of the Groninger Museum. I began to dream of a museum complex consisting of several pavilions to accommodate individual collections. Because the nature of each collection was so diverse (encompassing local history, eastern ceramics, old master paintings and contemporary art), it became evident that the best

Alessandro and Francesco Mendini, checked interior

solution would be to invite one architect to design each part.

Alessandro Mendini's experience in designing furniture in collaboration with other artists, designers and architects, suggested that he would be able to do the same on a much larger scale. After Mendini was appointed as Chief Architect for the project, we agreed on the role of great contrasts in the museum, not only in terms of design but in effectively attracting visitors from all over the world.

The criteria for the guest architects were that they should not have worked in a particularly post-modernist or traditional way and would preferably be artists from Asia, America and Europe. Those invited

initially were Shiro Kuramata, Philippe Starck and Frank Stella. Unfortunately, Kuramata could not accept the invitation and Frank Stella's plan could not be executed and so the guest architects became Michele de Lucchi, for the local history section, Philippe Starck, for Eastern ceramics, and Coop Himmelblau for the ancient art collection.

Mendini was responsible for the complete building and also designed the pavilion of contemporary art and the temporary exhibition space, in addition to the general functions such as the entrance hall, café, offices and library.

A year after the death of Rossini, Verdi conceived a *Requiem* in his honour. He

did not want this to be composed by himself alone but wished to involve 12 other Italian composers, indicating the parts which had to be solo, quartet, chorus etc, and who should compose each one.

This work was considered lost but was found recently. There was a première in 1986. I was struck by the similarity of Verdi's initiative for a *Requiem* to celebrate the exceptional composer, Rossini, and my concept for a museum as a reaction to the exceptional gift of *Gasunie*. Although there was some protest about the building prior to its construction, within three years of opening the new Groninger Museum has received over a million visitors from all over the world.

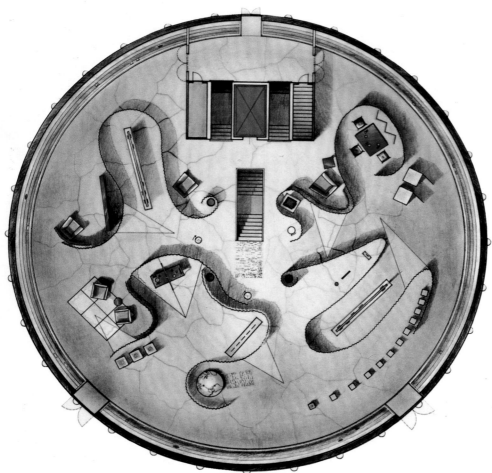

FROM ABOVE, L TO R: Philippe Starck,
Decorative Arts pavilion, display cases;
Alessandro and Francesco Mendini, mosaic
corridor; Philippe Starck, Decorative Arts
pavilion, plan

Michele de Lucchi, Regional Archaeology and History pavilion, display detail; BELOW: Alessandro & Francesco Mendini, Visual Arts pavilion (post-1950), interior

Alessandro and Francesco Mendini, Central Building, oval gallery; BELOW: Central Building, François Morellet's neon ceiling sculpture

Coop Himmelblau, Visual Arts (pre-1950), exhibition gallery; BELOW: Coop Himmelblau and Alessandro and Francesco Mendini, east wing exterior

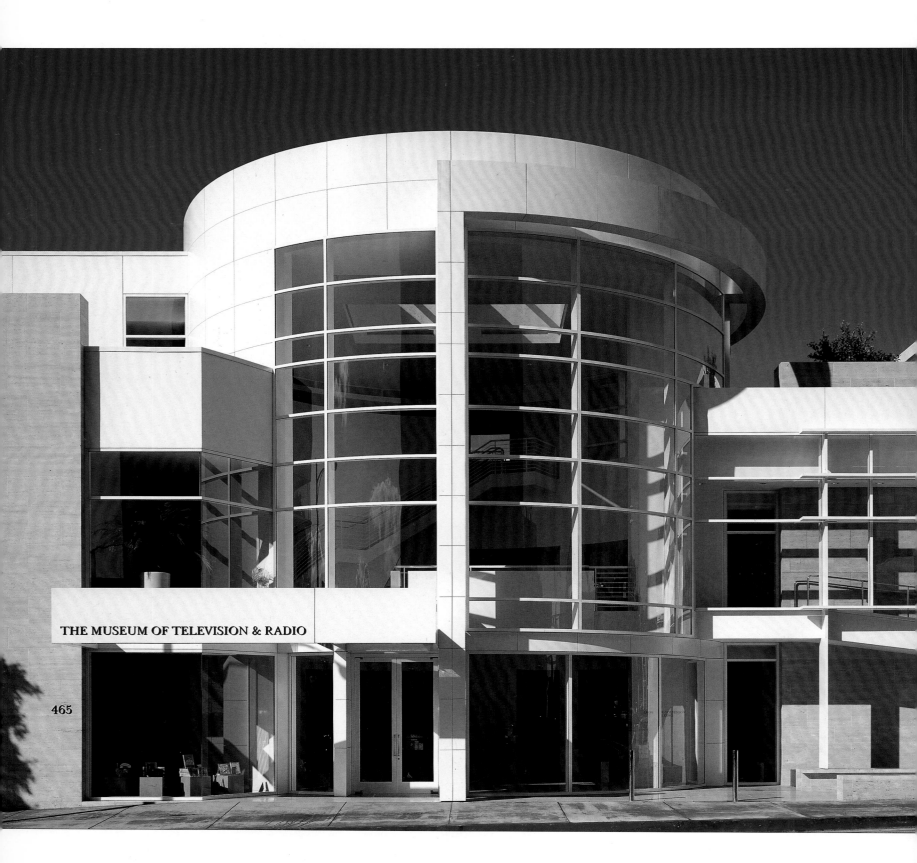

THE MUSEUM OF TELEVISION & RADIO

465

42

RICHARD MEIER & PARTNERS
MUSEUM OF TELEVISION & RADIO
Los Angeles

The site of the new California facility for the Museum of Television & Radio (1993-96) is prominently located at the south-west corner of the intersection of North Beverly Drive and Little Santa Monica Boulevard in Beverly Hills. It is filled with natural light and open to the street in a manner that is appropriate to the Southern California climate.

The two-storey building, which reuses much of the existing structure, is connected to an adjacent building that has been renovated for office space. The two facades on each of the public sides of the building are largely-transparent. They provide views to and from the street and sidewalk, for passerby and museum visitor alike, into the skylit rotunda lobby and gallery areas located on the ground floor.

The entry facade on North Beverly Drive is set back slightly from the property line to create a public forecourt leading to the double-height rotunda lobby. The skylit lobby serves as the radiant centre of the museum, providing direct access to the gallery area, 150-seat theatre, radio listening room, radio studio, multi-purpose education room, museum shop and information desk on the ground floor.

From the lobby, visitors circulate to the second floor via a stepped ramp which penetrates the exhibition area. This offers views back over the ground floor spaces before winding its way up to the library and video console room. The less public spaces, including the board of trustees' room, are located on the third floor, which is accessed via a circular stairway from the second floor. Also located on this top level is the roof garden which is used for receptions and outdoor events.

The skylit lobby, gallery area and promenade ramp, combined with large expanses of glass on the facades, create an open and vibrant environment for the museum. The exterior walls are clad in light-coloured natural stone, white metal panels, and clear glass, creating a harmonious relationship between the street and the museum's interiors.

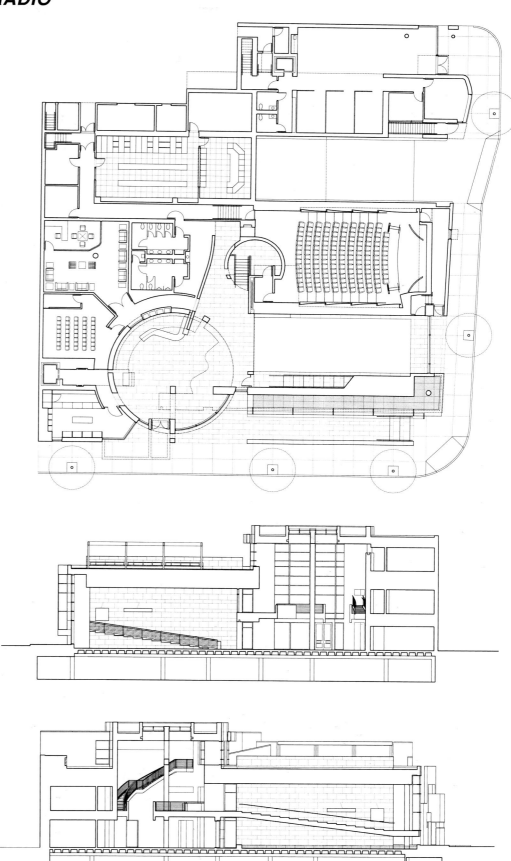

FROM ABOVE: First floor plan; sections

HANS HOLLEIN
GUGGENHEIM MUSEUM
Vienna

Hans Hollein, as prize-winner of an international competition, conceived this initial master plan for a new development across the Danube – the 'Donaucity'. An area (originally dedicated for a World Fair) was developed for office structure, housing and cultural buildings.

Existing highways are covered by a slab on which various buildings will be executed, including an elementary school which represents the corner of the 'Donaucity'. The Guggenheim Museum is inserted into the fabric of the new city and intersected by a diagonal walkway from the river. The axis creates a dynamic counterpart to the fractured shells of the new building which define the Guggenheim Plaza.

The museum itself utilises approximately 23,330 square metres of the site, with 11,000 square metres set aside for exhibition space (the core collection and temporary exhibits), arranged over the first, second and third levels. The auditorium is located below the first level where facilites are provided for parking, loading and storage.

In addition to exhibition space, the first level accommodates cloakroom, ticketing, and information areas and a museum shop and café, which are accessed from the Guggenheim Plaza. Another café is also located at a key point facing the river.

The second level is predominately exhibition space; likewise, the third floor. Here provision is also made for a library and seminar room in addition to another café and restaurant which are located in the wing projecting towards the river. This responds to the increased need for such facilities in today's museum, while maximising the inherent potential of the riverside location.

Model views

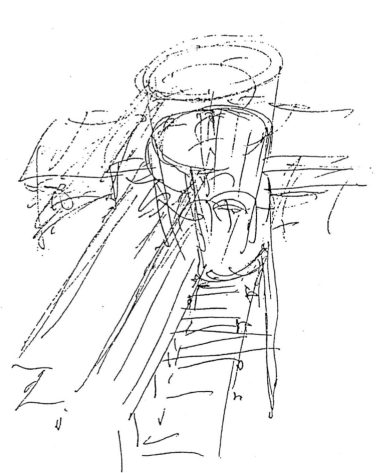

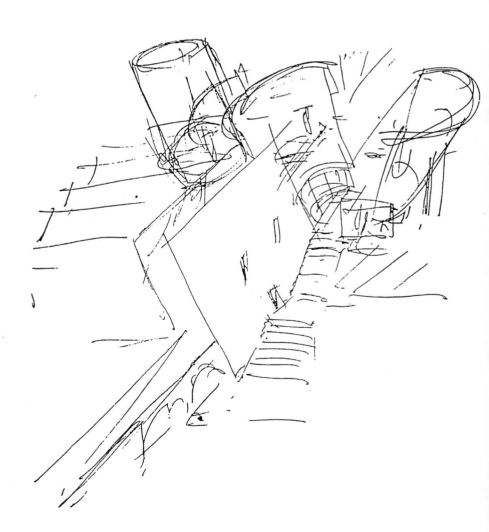

FROM ABOVE: Model views; Conceptual sketches

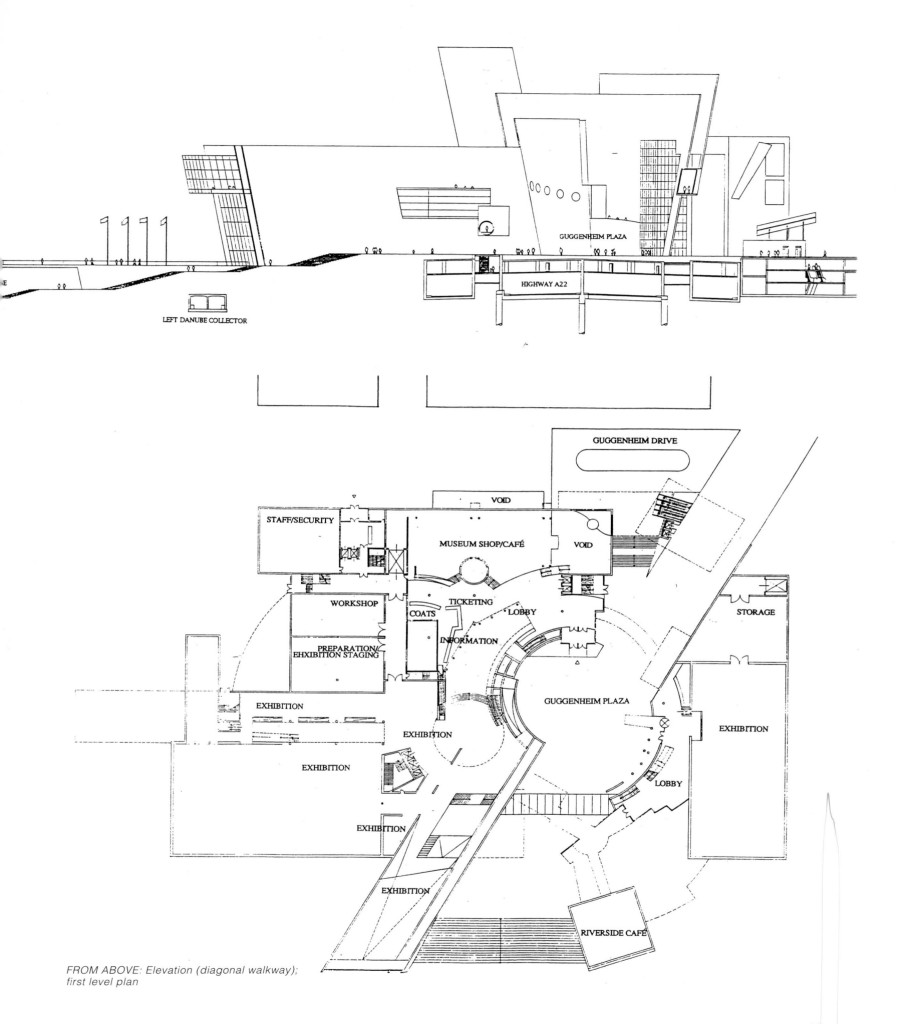

LEFT DANUBE COLLECTOR

HIGHWAY A22

GUGGENHEIM PLAZA

GUGGENHEIM DRIVE

VOID

STAFF/SECURITY

MUSEUM SHOP/CAFÉ

VOID

WORKSHOP

TICKETING

COATS

LOBBY

STORAGE

INFORMATION

PREPARATION/
EHXIBITION STAGING

EXHIBITION

EXHIBITION

GUGGENHEIM PLAZA

EXHIBITION

EXHIBITION

EXHIBITION

LOBBY

EXHIBITION

EXHIBITION

RIVERSIDE CAFÉ

*FROM ABOVE: Elevation (diagonal walkway);
first level plan*

THE EUROPEAN CENTRE OF VOLCANISM
St Ours-les-Roches, Auvergne

Volcanoes are a constant reminder of the ongoing process of formation of our planet. The European Centre of Volcanism, designed in 1994-96 (to be constructed over the next few years), relates to the curiosity of man and his search for knowledge but also to strong emotions about life and death, the creation of the earth, the birth of man; atavistic feelings are reflected in man's ambivalent attraction to fire as both a constructive and destructive force.

The deeply ritualistic and symbolic aspect associated with the idea of a centre of volcanism is strengthened by the museum's location in a natural setting dominated by the presence of extinct volcanoes. The characteristic shapes of the volcanoes demand an integral relationship between the building and its environment, while the nature of the theme suggested a subterranean development.

The European Centre of Volcanism has both scientific and emotional implications. The museum has to attract visitors of different interests, different ages and different educational backgrounds, so it is important that a visit to the Centre is not only educational but entertaining.

The message of volcanism will be conveyed both by the exhibition and the spatial and visual arrangements of the site and buildings, above ground and underground. The complex is designed to impress upon the visitor a variety of ideas and sensations in relation to volcanism.

There is no separation between the building and the landscape, nor between the underground and surface area; the distinctions between what is the container and the content are blurred. The complex is to be an unique creation, specific to this singular situation and must therefore convey a significant image that is clearly memorable and identifiable.

The theme of volcanoes is related in both a direct and metaphorical way. To enter the Centre people follow a processional path and descend into an abyss. The experience is evocative of a journey towards the centre of the Earth, with implications of reaching the underworld and of Jules Verne and Dante Alighieri's purgatory. It also refers to the womb and the protective cave.

The presence of fire symbolises magma and life springing forth. The atmosphere is at the same time sinister and threatening, and exuberant and joyful. Ashes are confronted with greenery.

In celebrating the link with volcanism and nature, the Centre also commemorates the Auvergne area. This is rich in volcanic traces of great beauty and has a special atmosphere due to volcanic materials, giving the buildings a specific character and feeling. The materials for the museum derive from the nature of the site: stone, grass, water.

When ascending to surface level, the visitor will be confronted with a spectacular view of the region. The imposing presence of the Auvergne volcanoes encourages more attention to be paid to volcanic objects and products – from the stone used for building the famous, local churches to the mineral water on the visitor's dining table.

OPPOSITE: Model view; ABOVE L TO R: Auvergne volcanoes; aerial view of projected site

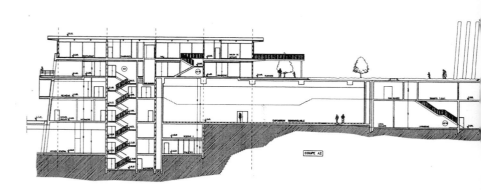

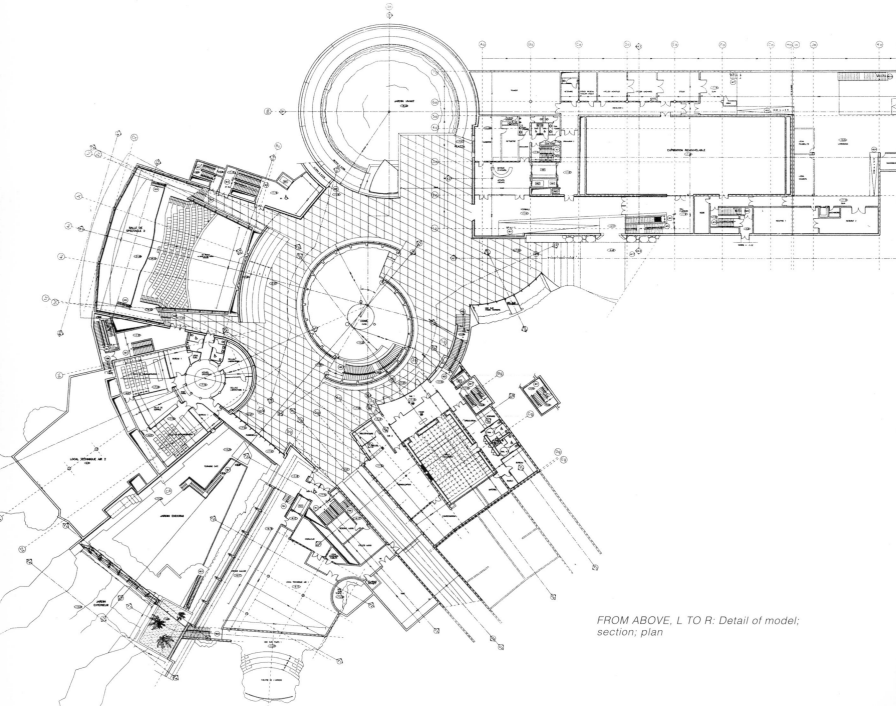

FROM ABOVE, L TO R: Detail of model; section; plan

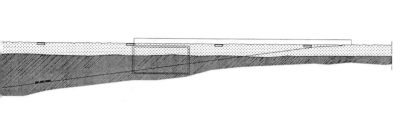

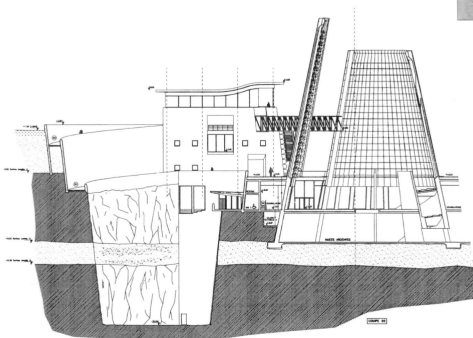

FROM ABOVE: Model views; section

KISHO KUROKAWA
SHIGA KOGEN ROMAN ART MUSEUM
Nagano, Japan

The Shiga Kogen Roman Art Museum, completed in 1996, is situated at the base of Uebayashi Ski Run in Shiga Kogen Ski Resort which is host to the Nagano Olympics. A small brook flows by the site which is located in an area of abundant natural beauty.

The town of Yamanouchi gave birth to the Chinese-style painter, Katei Kodama, and the museum houses some 70 pieces created by the artist and his school. In addition to this, it incorporates a collection of Edo, Meiji and Taisho era artefacts donated by the eminent artist Nobutaka Oka and his family. These are exhibited together with the collection of Roman and antique iridescent glass. Part of the Roman glass collection is placed in conical, glass cases that have been specially designed for the artefacts.

The two-storey structure is composed of reinforced concrete and wood. Its fragmented elliptical shape is effective in introducing elements of light, shadow, wind and landscape into the spatial composition. The gently sloping roof of the building has been designed in order to prevent the accumulation of snow.

The museum shop and café are housed in a transparent, cone-shaped structure. Although sponsored by the town, the art museum also benefits from the co-operation of local groups.

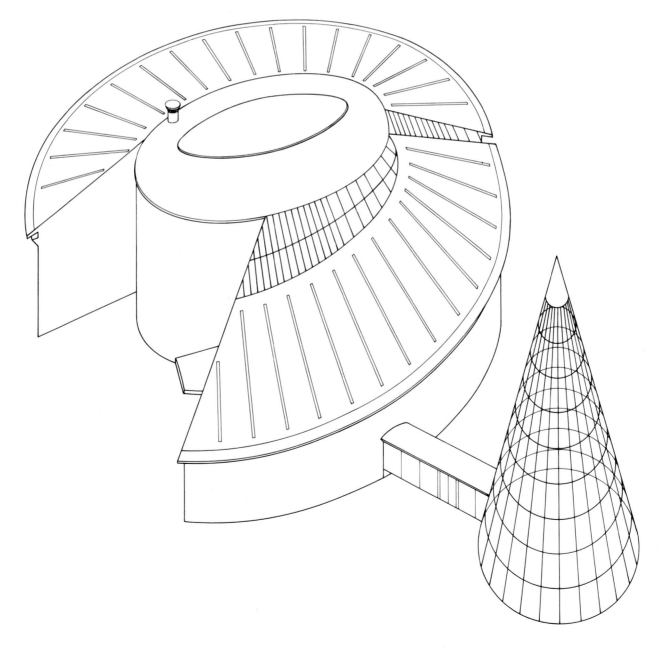

Axonometric

55

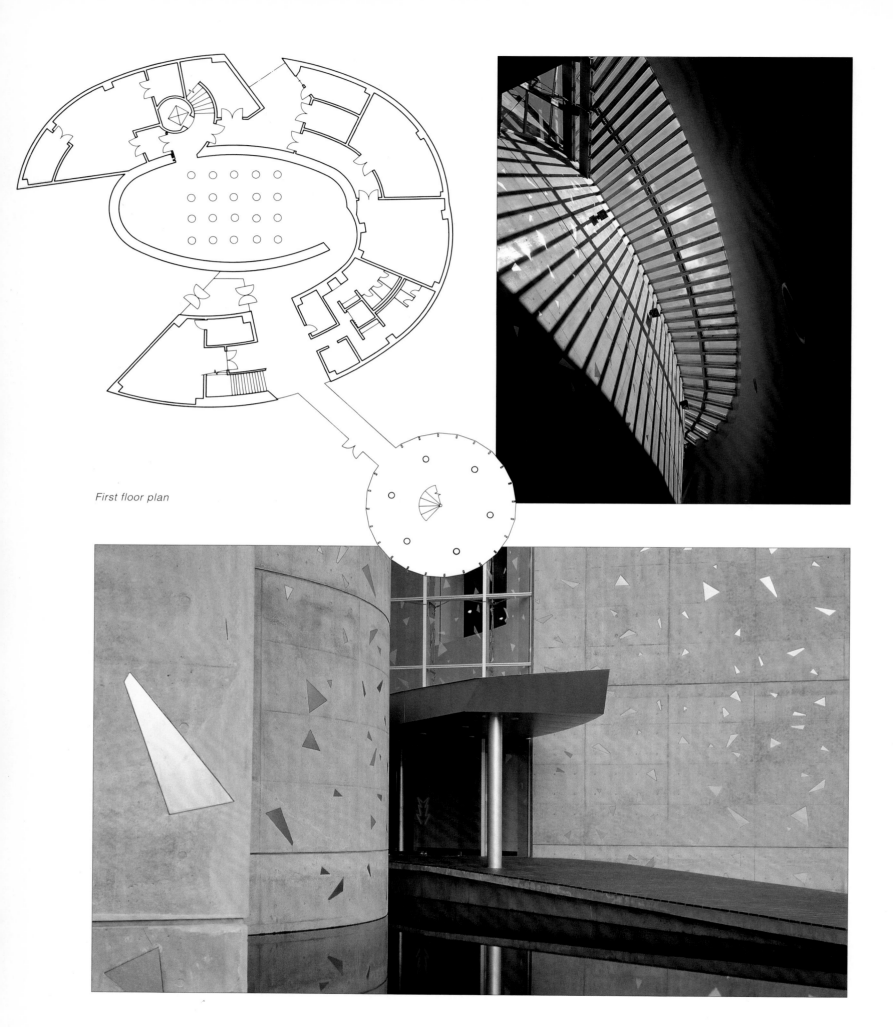

First floor plan

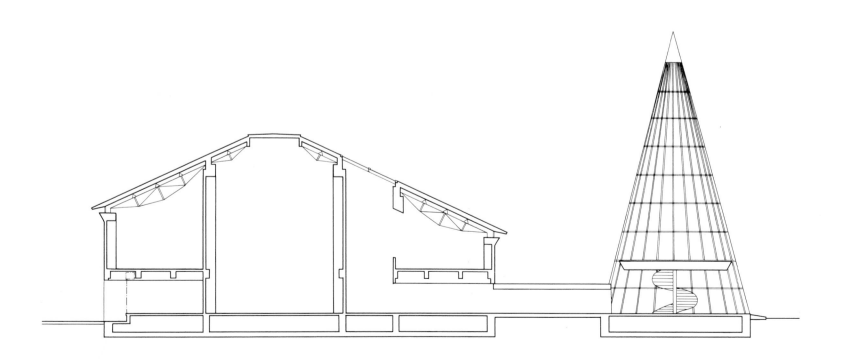

Section

57

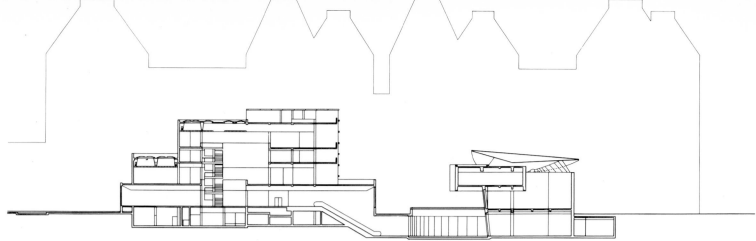

ABOVE: Section; BELOW: First basement floor plan

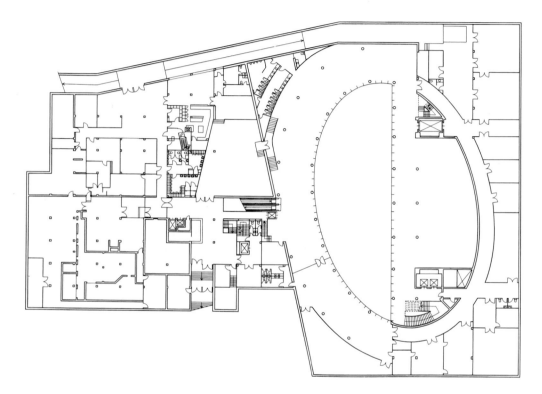

Photomontage of site with computer-generated image of new wing

NEW WING OF RIJKSMUSEUM VINCENT VAN GOGH
Amsterdam

The new wing was proposed as an extension of Rijksmuseum Vincent Van Gogh (National Museum), in response to the dramatic increase in visitors and future privatisation. The site is located in the Museumplein of Amsterdam in The Netherlands.

The extension (designed in 1990-95), will be constructed on the opposite side of the entrance hall of the main museum, by the park. The Museumplein is an important heart of the city and this was given careful consideration by the design of the new wing: two storeys are planned above ground level and the remainder is to be accommodated below, effectively scaling down the volume of the extension.

The new Stedelijk Museum (City Museum), which is located close-by, will be extended to the park side. The plan-ning of the whole park has been under-taken by Sven-Ingvar Anderson, a Danish landscape architect.

Abstract interrelation
Rijksmuseum Vincent Van Gogh was the last work of Gerrit van Rietveld (1888-1964), one of the founders of CIAM (Congrès Internationaux d'Architecture Moderne). He passed away during the planning stage of this work but the museum was completed in accordance with his design.

While adopting Rietveld's characteris-tic geometry, the new wing expresses its own identity by making use of the ellipti-cal form. A path connects the main museum and extension beneath ground level, introducing an invisible relationship to the scheme.

Asymmetry
The crescent shape adopted for the new wing has been slightly tilted on the side facing the courtyard. The semi-circular, underground courtyard provides a water garden which can be considered an abstract quotation of the Japanese garden. At ground level the structure is surrounded with an elliptical-shaped pond.

The mezzanine floor of the square Exhibition Hall houses a collection of Japanese *ukiyoe* (art depicting the pleasure quarters of 17th- and 18th-century Japan) which were collected by Van Gogh himself. Here, the axis is slightly shifted.

The use of asymmetrical devices is a way of expressing the sophisticated Japanese tradition.

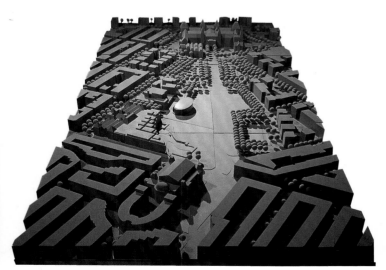

Model detail and general view

FUKUI CITY MUSEUM OF ART
Fukui, Japan

The Fukui City Museum of Art, completed in 1996, was designed to provide the people of Fukui city with a place in which to appreciate art. It offers an opportunity to engage in creative activity, while contributing to the revival of local artistic activities and the development of art and culture. The museum realises Fukui's goal of 'recognising the artistic legacy of Fukui city and developing it for the future'.

The city required a combined fine art exhibition and performance art facility. The brief requested a fine art exhibition space in which to house a permanent exhibition of the works of the late sculptor Hiroatsu Takada, in addition to a facility for other exhibitions and an atelier open to the public. The performing arts facility was also to include a library for material on the life of the actor Shigeyoshi Uno (who was born in Fukui) and an auditorium, to be planned in the future.

The site is located on the outskirts of the city, adjacent to a park of approximately 4 hectares in area. The architecture of the museum was required to blend in with the greenery of the park, which was to be incorporated into the facility as much as possible. Accordingly, the exhibition facility is a low structure that is situated in the centre of the complex. The performance art facility is a higher structure situated on the eastern side of the site. Between these two facilities there is a three-storey communal entrance hall, a cafeteria, and a lecture auditorium.

All of the gallery passageways are connected to exterior exhibition spaces and the park, creating an intermediate space between nature and the building. The height of the exhibition space is limited to two storeys by incorporating the storage areas below ground level. This prevents the building from becoming an obstruction when viewed from the park.

The exhibition spaces are located on the first and second floors, exploiting the unity of the fine art exhibition space and the surrounding park. The atelier is designed so that it may also serve as an exhibition space: a one- or two-storey open area above the gallery passage-ways. The information exchange room and the cafeteria are set in a location that provides an open view of the park. The passage from the first to the second floor in the lobby can be connected by either a spiral ramp or an elevator, providing easy access for the handicapped.

The volume of the performing arts facility (which is to be constructed later) is not yet determined. However, it wll be based on providing a performance hall that can seat 1,000 people, a library and rehearsal areas.

The entire structure is sheathed with a glass curtain wall. Accordingly, double-framed glass, sealed heat-deflecting sashes, and semi-opaque heat- and light-deflecting rolling blinds are incorporated in the scheme to control the effects of hot and cold weather. Penetration of the direct rays of the sun is reduced by constructing the exterior walls at an angle of approximately 15 degrees. The curved wall, which brings to mind fractal geometry, is an example of Kisho Kurokawa's abstract symbolism.

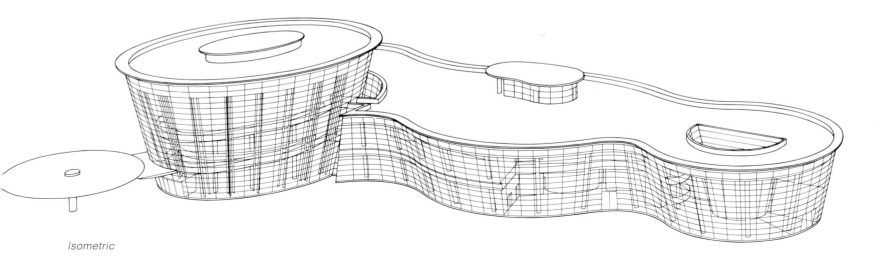

Isometric

FOSTER AND PARTNERS

AMERICAN AIR MUSEUM IN BRITAIN
Duxford

In 1986, Foster and Partners was approached by the Imperial War Museum to design a building to display its collection of American aircraft at Duxford near Cambridge, one of the many wartime air bases in East Anglia from which the American Airforce played its crucial role.

The building has been designed to offer a neutral backdrop to the aircraft. Simple in form, with an emphasis on clarity, natural light and an economic system of atmospheric control, its drama lies in the broad curve of its roof, and in the abrupt slice of its 90-metre-long, 18.5-metre-high glazed south-east facade which offers views out to the airfield, runways and beyond.

Amongst the 20 aircraft in the collection is the vast B52 bomber. It is so dominant that its 16-metre-high tail fin and 61-metre wingspan were the key influence on the form of the building, which is based on an arched geometric shape – the torus – and is elliptical in plan.

The single-span vault, the largest of its type in Europe, rises at the building's fully glazed south-east elevation to accommodate the tail plain of the B52, and falls gently back towards the north-west where it is partially dug right into the landscape. This unusual roof structure was developed with Ove Arup & Partners using only five geometries of pre-cast panels repeated through its form.

A basic function of the building is to protect the aircraft from further environmental damage – many had suffered through long-term exposure to the elements. For the purposes of conservation, humidity levels were more important than temperature, so that while the thermal mass of the concrete structure insulates against major variations in temperature – and removes the need for both air conditioning and heating – a simple dehumidifying system achieves a relative humidity level of 50-55 per cent, well below the critical 65 per cent level at which aluminium begins to deteriorate. The glazed south-east elevation filters UV rays, preventing discoloration.

Visitors approach the museum from the north-west. They emerge from a tunnel-like entrance to find themselves midway in the volume of space, facing the nose of the B52 Stratofortress. Around and beyond the enormous B52, they can survey a panorama of aircraft on every scale, some suspended from the roof, and some on the floor below, before proceeding with their tour.

The aeroplanes in the collection date from the First World War to the Gulf War. Many of the aircraft in the Imperial War Museum's collection at Duxford, are still operational. This is not a static museum, and from inside the new building, through the glazed facade, people can watch the daily movement and flight of historic aircraft.

After 18 months of construction, and 11 years of fund-raising (including private donations from veteran American airmen), the American Air Museum in Britain was opened by HM The Queen in August 1997.

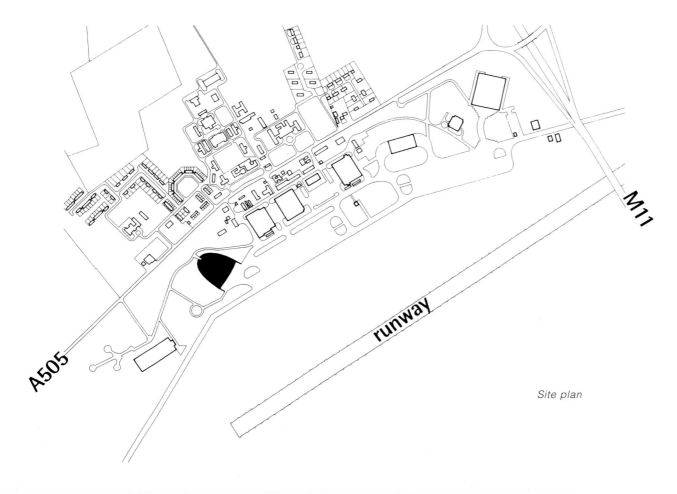

Site plan

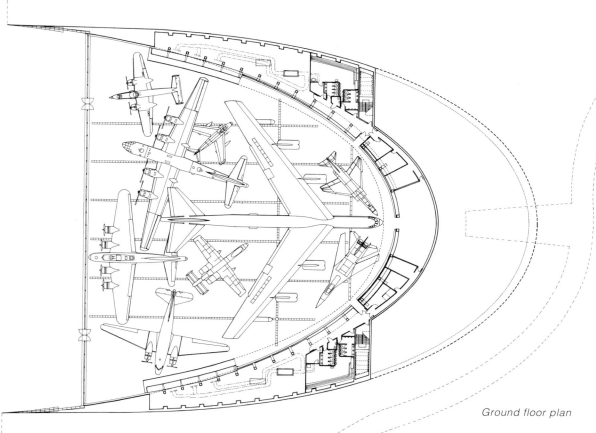

Ground floor plan

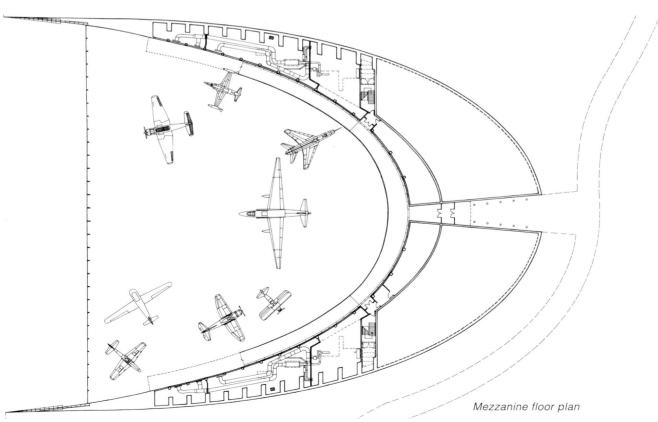

Mezzanine floor plan

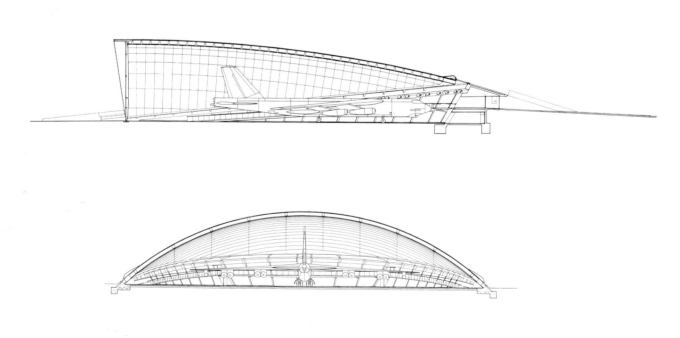

*FROM ABOVE: Longitudinal section;
cross section*

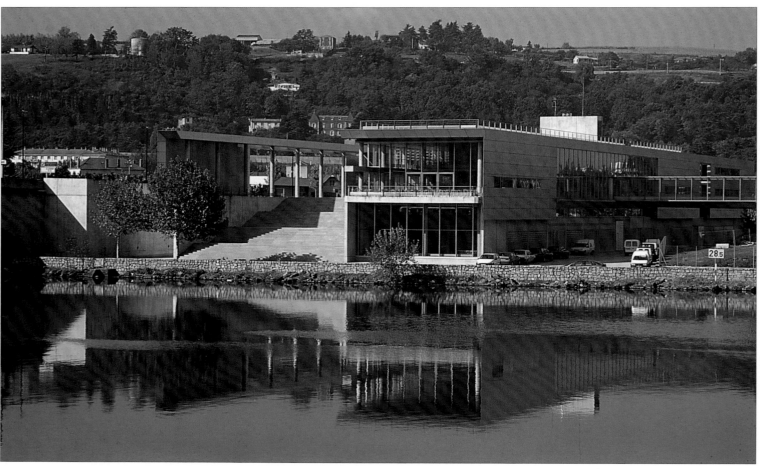

CHAIX MOREL AND ASSOCIATES
SAINT-ROMAIN-EN-GAL ARCHAEOLOGICAL MUSEUM
Saint-Romain-en-Gal, France

This project developed from three main considerations. The first of these was the search for a solid, rich urban site at the other end of the bridge, facing the direction of Vienna. This lies between the bridge and the museum and comprises a vast staircase and square extending downwards towards the Rhône and up to the belvedere which overlooks the whole of the site. It is also a feature of the landscape which characterises and emphasises the museum.

The second consideration was that the proximity of the Rhône (the origin of the Roman settlement) encouraged key parts of the museum – ie, most of the public areas – to be located by the river. These areas are therefore linked in turn to the archaeological site and the river.

Thirdly, to achieve the maximum degree of transparency in the organisation of the space and to limit the confinement of the building (which is built on archaeological remains), a solution based on three main elements was chosen in this initial phase:
– the belvedere staircase (triangular in form and tangential to the road and the bridge) extends northwards in the form of a platform, housing the storerooms and workshops for mosaic restoration in the lower level;
– a transparent, linear gallery is set on to this platform. The gallery comprises the reception area, the temporary exhibition and the Archaeological Research Centre (ARC). It is positioned at an oblique angle so as to orientate all of these areas towards the archaeological site;
– the permanent exhibition is set up in the quietest area of the site, on the archaeological excavation to the north. The location immediately reflects the concept which is central to the Saint-Romain-en-Gal museum, namely: an on-site museum with ongoing archaeological excavations. It is therefore a growing, developing museum.

On the basis of these three factors, the areas within the museum have been divided up very simply. The reception area is reached from the square located at road level, midway on the belvedere staircase. The cafeteria, which is adjacent to the reception area, has a balcony overlooking the Rhône. The temporary exhibitions open out on to the archaeological site and extend on to a patio area that separates the museum from the Archaeological Research Centre (ARC). The conference room and area for preservation work are situated beneath the staircase.

A footbridge crosses the rue de la Chantrerie and leads to the permanent exhibition site. The entire lower level is taken up by the museum stores, the ARC store, the workshop for mosaic restoration, and the technical and service departments. All of these areas are built around a large central circulation which is accessible to store handling equipment and leads into the service area. The workshop for mosaic restoration is situated in the far western part of the building.

The project offers contrasting views of the museum. On the south facade, the framework screening the building from the sun, at an angle to the conservation offices, extends to the bridge and creates a penetrable boundary between the road and square. This part of the building provides vast areas of transparency within the reception and cafeteria, and towards the permanent exhibition and the archaeological site.

When viewed from the embankment and from Vienna, the museum has a very distinct outline characterised by the staircase, the terrace and the cafeteria at the prow of the gallery, and also the aerial dimensions of the permanent exhibition.

The permanent exhibition consists of a vast platform built over the remains currently being excavated. This immediately establishes a distinct relationship with the archaeological site as a whole, and with the excavation which is contained within and protected by the building. In the long term, these archaeological remains could easily become an integrated part of the permanent exhibition, simply through the creation of vertical circulation and an external shell.

For the construction of the museum the architects have opted for the lightest medium in order to minimise the foundations. The use of metal makes it possible to span a distance of approximately 20 metres, thus limiting the number of anchor points to 24. Furthermore, the modular structure means that the building will be easily extendable at a later date without any alterations to its character. The structure, which serves as an observation and work platform, is more in keeping with the lightweight constructions used on archaeological sites than that of a solid building, which would threaten to draw attention away from the archaeological remains.

The permanent exhibition platform which opens out on to the site and the Rhône, is an extremely flexible structure, which will enable the museum to develop in any number of directions in the future. The cyma featured on this platform are arranged in a pattern reminiscent of the archaeological remains in the lower level. Openings give visitors a view of the excavation and supply natural light to the lower level. The arrangement of the cyma creates a differentiated scale of the areas, and their dark, neutral surface confirms the museographic primitiveness of the extremely rich site content, particularly the mosaics.

Developments include the organisation of the museum and the permanent exhibition space around a linear central area and sub-areas, each corresponding to a different theme (water, exchanges, economy etc). This new layout offers a dual approach to the exhibition. In the reception area, a model of the museum, provides visitors with a synthetic representation of the museographic complex, the site and the museum. From the reception, visitors can follow a circuit which guides them through the different themes. They will then reach the mezzanine floors, from where they will obtain a more open, aerial view of the mosaics. The entire permanent exhibition takes the form of a metal structure based on micro-piling at an angle to the walls of the remains.

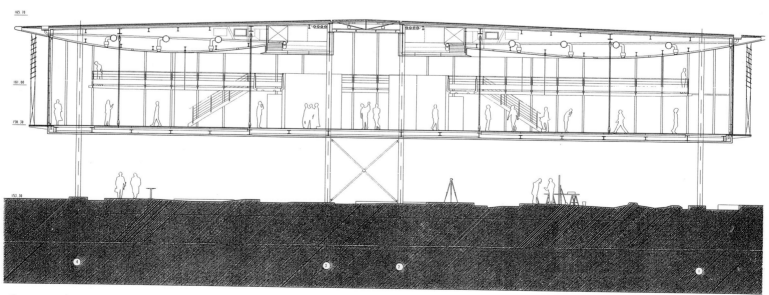

Cross section

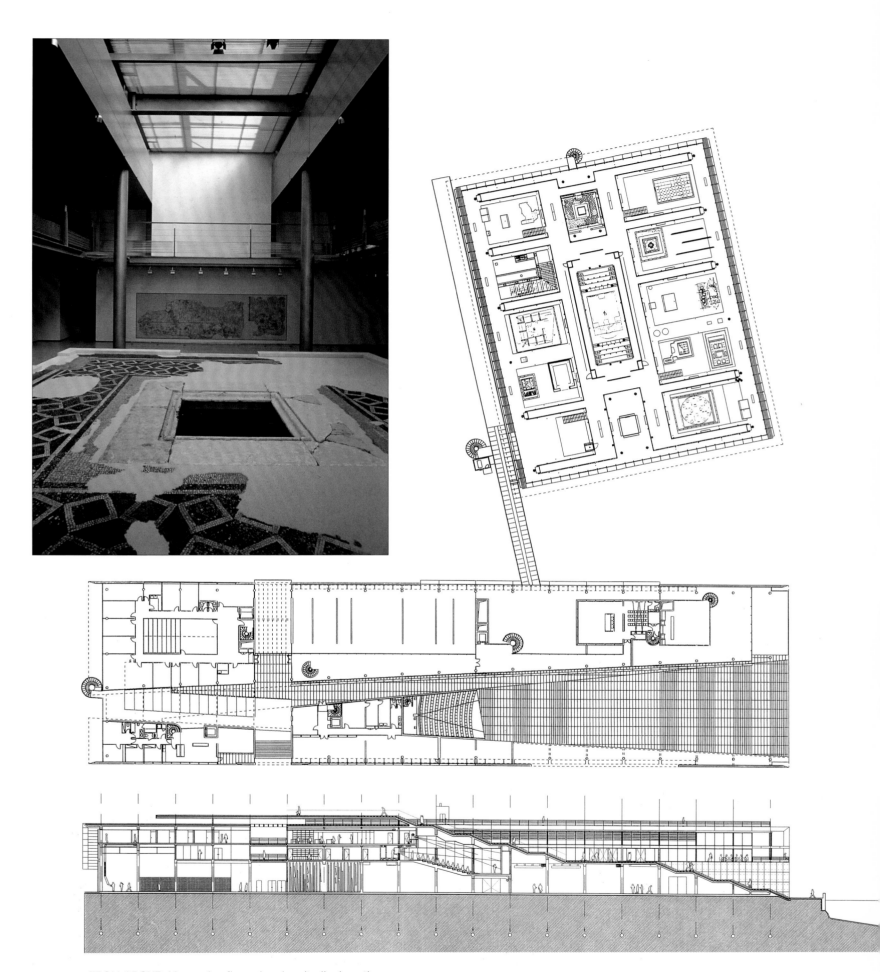

FROM ABOVE: Mezzanine floor plan; longitudinal section

BENSON + FORSYTH

In November 1991, Benson and Forsyth addressed a packed Mackintosh lecture theatre on their recent competition win for the new Museum of Scotland (which will be completed in 1998). Here, Gordon Benson expands on the practice's recent work and the threads which bind it together.

The three projects illustrated here were generated by similar preoccupations. They draw upon and reflect the forces and circumstances which created their immediate surroundings; the broader tradition and forms in their regional context; their specific functional requirements.

The intention of the Edinburgh project is that these references and responses will be fully absorbed into the building. Their purpose is to ensure a subliminally appropriate fit between the collection and its container, and between the container and the city. In short, the subtext assumes its conventional role in relation to the narrative, use and operation of the building as a shelter and home for the collection.

In the Japanese projects the situation is reversed in that the subtext becomes the text. This unfamiliar circumstance arises directly out of the brief.

Arata Isozaki, was invited by the prefecture of Toyama in north-west Japan to advise them on an appropriate monument to commemorate their 1992 Expo. In the wake of the Osaka Follies, in which Isozaki had been instrumental, he recommended seven European architects to the prefecture and suggested that they should be invited to build permanent buildings in 14 towns, rather than a monument or temporary pieces as at Osaka. The selection of European architects was significant in that the Japanese were looking for an alternative perspective on their culture and traditions, in order to transcend the North American perception of 'progress', imported after 1945.

The functional requirements of both of the projects, in which the practice is involved, are relatively straightforward; a monument to time in Oshima and the conversion and extension of traditional store houses, in order to display the domestic collections of the residents of Jyohanna. The unwritten brief was that the buildings should examine and make explicit the relationship between tradition and the present, and the prevailing, blanket notion of 'progress'. The duality of convention and invention posed in the artist's obligation to both history and innovation is, of course, something with which we, as Europeans, have been preoccupied since the Enlightenment.

National Museum of Scotland, Edinburgh – framed views, Administration Building

THE NATIONAL MUSEUM OF SCOTLAND
Edinburgh

The National Museum of Scotland is located to the south of the Old Town, opposite Greyfriars Graveyard and adjacent to the Royal Museum of Scotland, designed by Francis Fowke in 1861. The upper floors of the new building will have magnificent views of Edinburgh Castle and the ridge of the Old Town to the north and Arthur's Seat and Salisbury Crags to the south-east.

Conversely, the building will be fully visible and a significant land-mark from Calton Hill or the public terrace of the castle esplanade. The site is flanked by the medieval field roads, leading into Edinburgh from the south, Candlemaker Row and Forrest Road; and the orthogonal geometries of the 19th-century George IV Bridge and Chambers Street.

The brief called for a building which would be fully integrated with, and entered through, the existing museum. The new building would therefore have to reconcile the change of scale and expression between Fowke's building, which is one of the few horizontally organised buildings in Edinburgh, and the diminutive, vertically organised houses clustered around Greyfriars.

This is achieved by wrapping a lower, outer building, containing the study galleries and the temporary exhibition space and following the precise undulations of the field roads, around the higher, rectilinear, main gallery and the triangular entrance space.

The organisation is reminiscent of the castle's curtain-wall and keep, whilst the juxtaposition of the plastic outer wall with the formal geometry and axiality of the main gallery mediates between the Old and New Towns, whose respective characteristics both overlay the site.

The perimeter wall is the same height as the main frontage of the Royal Museum but is rotated away from the axis. The corner of Chambers Street is redefined by a cylinder which addresses the five approach roads and signals the presence of the two museums.

Functionally, the cylinder provides the non-specific gallery space, where direct connections could be made between the collection and the city. Formally, the cylinder echoes the half-moon battery of the castle, with its linear opening frames, and completes one reading of Fowke's building from Chambers Street; as two cubic pavilions linked by a lower, recessed colonnade.

Thus, Chambers Street is rearticulated as a square, forming an appropriate, formal approach to the existing, figural

North-south section

building, and reclaimed as the public space originally envisaged by Fowke. It would be pedestrianised, landscaped with trees and archaeological fragments, and would function both as an extension and forecourt to the two museums.

Internally, the entrance to the new museum is on the main axis of Fowke's magnificent, luminous hall. A second connection is made by extending the line of the colonnade into the base of the triangulated hall, which is conceived as a terminal space, concluding the act of entry. A large penetration through the outer wall at the focus of this space, addresses the entrance to Greyfriars opposite. The space itself is seen both as a displaced fragment of Fowke's hall and as a glass-roofed Edinburgh court, surrounded by a series of buildings, each with its own entrance.

The brief contained a dual ambition. It was considered imperative that the collection could be viewed as a whole, but also that individual components could be accessed directly. Consequently,

it is possible from the entrance space to embark on the chronological journey or to move directly into the three primary compartments.

The collection is extremely diverse and varies substantially in scale, from jewellery to standing stones, or from the Monymusk Reliquary to an oil rig. The intention is therefore to provide a range of galleries which is functionally appropriate and able to reflect the character and nature of the collection; the container reflects the contained and, in turn, the city in which it, itself, is contained.

In broad terms, the layers of the building are used to characterise the different elements of the collection. The lower ground floor is a crypt-like space with standing stones, graves and cysts, placed directly upon, or cut into the virgin rock. The ground floor houses material from the medieval church and kingship. The exhibits are displayed in niches carved out of the massive walls.

The upper three floors contain industrial archaeology and the 20th-century

display. The space is like an industrial machine hall, with a lighter, framed structure and voids which soar up to the boat-shaped roof and clerestory.

The roof terrace came into being as a response to four considerations: how to terminate the journey around the collection; how to connect the interior to the magnificent views of the city; how to present the building to the city, and how to maintain a stable internal environment and control the penetration of sunlight.

By placing selected archaeological and geological fragments on the roof terrace they could be viewed in a natural landscape of Scottish grasses, shrubs and wild flowers, rather than the decontextualised environment of a museum interior.

The roof terrace, or 'hanging valley', occupies a unique position as a mediator between the major elements of the city's natural landscape. Instantly recognisable from the castle esplanade, it would also be, arguably, the most significant urban elevation of the museum: a new monument on the Edinburgh skyline.

LEFT TO RIGHT: Model view, south elevation; interior of 18th-19th-century church, south wing

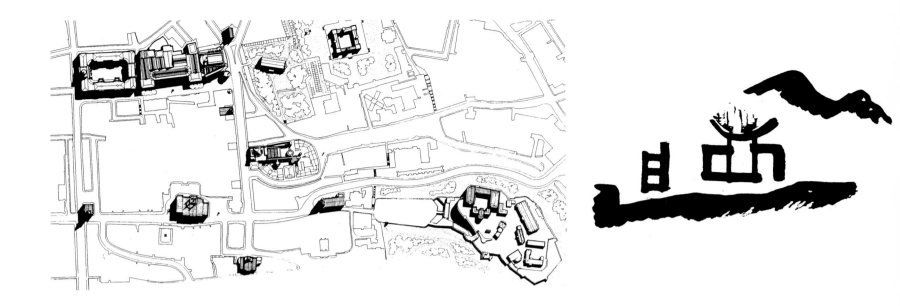

LEFT TO RIGHT: Site plan; Sketch of 'hanging valley'
roof garden; BELOW: Model view, north elevation

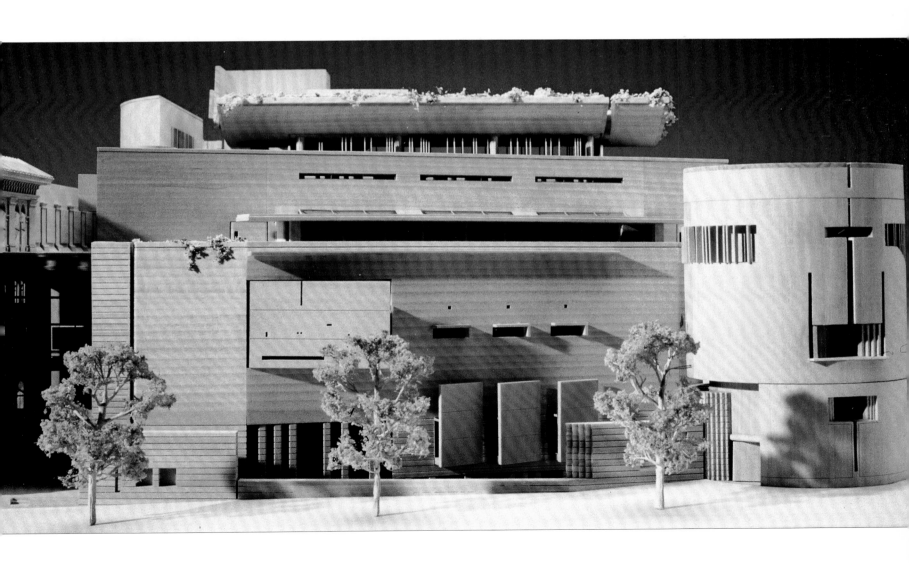

THE 'DIVIDED HOUSE'
Oshima, Japan

Oshima is located in the middle of a vast alluvial plain and is indistinguishable from its neighbouring towns. It has no beginning and no end. Beneath the surface, however, it is possible to unearth an older pattern of clusters of traditional dwellings located on slightly higher ground and surrounded by rice fields and exquisite frames for growing loofahs and drying rice grass. This agrarian pattern now co-exists with the 'progress' of the chemical plant, the car factory and the fashionable but inelegant blockwork houses.

The 'Divided House' project, which was completed in 1993, is an attempt to juxtapose the past and the present. The piece is divided by a wall which is aligned with the Pole Star. This establishes the longitude of the site and may be used with a nocturnal to measure the mean solar time at night. The angle of the stair within the wall establishes the latitude of the site. Cities on the same latitude are: San Francisco, Washington DC, Malaga, Algiers, Syracuse and Rhodes.

The wall divides the traditional crafts and agrarian occupation of the land from the products of industrialisation and of pure reason; the cylinder and the cube. The experiential synthesis of the 'past and present' can only be achieved by moving through the whole piece; in other words, by the passage of time. The fragments represent the head and tail sides of the coin which is Japan and the planet today.

A series of pre-mechanical devices for the measurement of time is built into the wall: the oil lamp, the charcoal box, the candle, the sand timer, the water timer and finally, within the cube, the human heartbeat.

STOREHOUSE MUSEUM
Jyohanna, Japan

Jyohanna is situated within a landscape of contrast. The grid of the town sits on a sloping spur eroded at the confluence of two rivers. The spur, in turn, sits on a plain, a grid of fields, defined by the curvilinear form of the Tatiyama Mountains. At all scales there is an inherent counterpoint between rectilinearity and free-form, between man and nature. It was a sophisticated understanding of these polarities and the poetic possibilities in re-relating them that formed the basis of the finest traditional architecture of the region.

A 15th-century temple complex of astonishing refinement and beauty is located on an escarpment at the edge of the town, forming a clearly articulated, collective grouping. It unfolds into awe-inspiring juxtapositions of built fabric, manicured gardens, and the rock of the mountain.

In contrast, the remainder of the town is impoverished: the existing Float Museum and the storehouses are all inward-looking, unrelated elements and the main square lacks definition and character. The opportunity existed to create a coherent place from which to explore the town, a *Machi-no-Kao* for Jyohanna.

The square is given definition by the articulation of entry from street to square, Float Museum to square, and square to Storehouse Museum. An undulating screen, reinforced by tree planting, defines the northern edge and picks up the line of the temple outcrop.

The square is well placed to become a natural fulcrum for both residents and visitors. It could be a place to learn about the town, its history and places of interest. It could also act as a focus for a series of walks, and a café could serve the needs of both museums as well as evening use.

The space and the elements which define and enclose the Storehouse Museum itself, may be seen as a series of varying responses to the traditional architecture of the storehouses and the town of Jyohanna. It has at the same moment both a sense of strangeness, and of being rooted in its location. It is hoped that this kaleidoscopic quality of what is 'normal' and 'new' will be stimulating and will allow those who know Jyohanna to see the familiar afresh.

The alterations to the storehouses themselves are minimal and are intended to fulfil two functions: to allow the three separate buildings to be linked so that they can function as a single entity and to reveal the fabric of the storehouses by 'peeling away' sections of the floor and wall finish to reveal the construction.

In common with these buildings, the new 'Galleria' displays a clear, structural articulation of column, beam and purlin but it does make a deliberate contrast in terms of form. The traditional role of the heavy roof enclosure and light screen walls is inverted so that the wall, although lightweight in terms of fabric, has a thickness which contains stairs, niches and is inhabited, while the roof is a louvered glass screen.

The tradition of spatial organisation based on a strict adherence to rectilinear geometry with, in the case of the storehouses, a strong sense of cellularity, is deliberately contrasted with the space of the Galleria and by asymmetries in both plan and section.

Thus, the past is to be seen in terms of the present and vice versa. The creation of such a synthesis offers a platform for progress, a new route to the future which does not deny the past.

SØREN ROBERT LUND

ARKEN MUSEUM OF MODERN ART
Copenhagen

The architects received the commission to design the museum after winning a national competition in 1988. The building was completed and opened eight years later, on 22 March 1996. The evolution of the design over this period has had a critical effect on the final building which stands today.

The design of the museum can be divided into a number of different realms, encompassing the overall layout, the spatial experience and, ultimately, the details.

The landscape and the building
Central to the design of the museum was the desire to create an interaction between the building and the existing coastal landscape with its beaches, harbours and lakes. The scale and character of the landscape were used as a starting point for the design, which culminates in a sculptural, horizontal building with different structural elements that stretch out, visually conquering the surrounding landscape.

By using the metaphor of the ship-wreck in the design, it is inscribed into the history of the landscape. The meta-phor was exploited as a creative starting point for the design, rather than a formal element, and acts as a narrative device in the public experience of the building.

Spatiality of the building
The spatiality of the museum is composed through the character of each space – its proportion, shape, light, acoustics etc – and its connection or contrast to the following spaces.

The museum is centred around a long, curved, axis and the surrounding land-scape is embraced by extending three additional, staggered, axes. The entrance is placed on the west side of the building, at which point the visitors have two choices: either to move from the outer foyer into the Art-axis, or to the main foyer. This creates a contrast between the intimate experience of the narrow entrance space and the vast expanse of the surrounding landscape; the metaphor being the porch of a medieval church.

The outer foyer is situated between the curved walls of the Art-axis and the main foyer. The principal steel construction penetrates the room like a spine with outstretched ribs. There is a sense of the structural lines crossing between the two walls. Beneath the outer foyer are situated the restrooms. Here we experience the contrast between the cave-like wardrobe area, with its ruby-red painted walls and black floor, and the white terrazzo-covered toilets, where the two-ton terrazzo sink is the visual centre.

The main foyer is given its character by the presence of a domed skylight, an arched outer wall (like a medieval perimeter wall), and the intersection of a steel footbridge that physically connects the balcony in the main axis with the restaurant on the second floor. To mark this point a 36-ton Norwegian granite block is situated in the entrance of the main foyer. The foyer, as a consequence, is defined not by its own space but by the elements that intersect and inhabit it.

From the main foyer there is access to the cinema and theatre. Both of these rooms have a cave-like character; conveyed by the shape, the technical design and the colours. As a result, the rooms contrast with the naturally-lit galleries.

The main gallery is the Art-axis, which is approximately 150-metres long and the unifying gallery in the composition; one wall is crescent-shaped, the other remains straight. Notionally, the space acts as the nave of the cathedral. From the Art-axis one has direct access to the galleries. To the south, one descends to the lower level of the museum which contains a gallery for graphic art.

The galleries to the north are defined by two skylights that underline the modular character of these spaces. Both skylights are designed to the proportion of 1:3 (height:width). This module is reflected throughout the rest of the building, from the design of the steelwork to the two bay windows situated beside each skylight. Here the interaction between the interior and the view out to the landscape, presented by the bay-windows, allows true expression of one of the principal design ideas.

The Red-axis bisects the building, stretching from the main foyer to the boat-bridge at the harbour. Seen as a structural element, it is one of the most important pieces of the building, creating a visual interaction with the interior and exterior. The intimate character of the space is emphasised by the tilting walls, the ruby-red colours and the black floor.

From the Red-axis we proceed to the restaurant on the second floor. This is the climax of the journey through the building. It is through the individual interaction of the structural elements and this cli-matic view to the sea that the experience finds its character. The main structure of the restaurant resembles that of the outer foyer, with the spine-like steel gutter and steel beams stretched out like ribs.

Materiality and details
Throughout the design of the museum the materiality and details have been driven by the layout of the building and the metaphorical connection with the character of the coastal landscape. The landscape is defined by its poetic roughness, which the texture of the museum attempts to convey. As a consequence, the main material employed is concrete cast *in situ*, accompanied on the exterior by steel facades. These materials are carried through to the interior with white concrete floors, steel beams and steel doors. The joints of the beams and doors are visible, along with coupling-bolts inspired by 19th-century cast-iron design.

80

Developmental sketches

AKIRA KURYU & ASSOCIATES
UEMURA NAOMI MEMORIAL MUSEUM
Hidaka, Japan

Uemura Naomi (born in 1941) was a world-famous adventurer who challenged long distance exploration. Not only did he complete a solo 12,000-kilometre dog-sled trip through the Arctic region but he was the first person in the world to scale the highest peaks of five continents. Unfortunately, Uemura failed to return after a solo winter ascent of Mount McKinley in 1984. He was 43-years old.

The Uemura Naomi Memorial Museum is located in his birthplace, Hidaka (formerly Kaminogo), in Hyogo Prefecture. The museum, which was completed in 1994, is constructed as a memorial centre to give testimony to his bold achievements. The district is surrounded by old mountains with rich greenery and ridge lines; rice fields are prepared elaborately in terraces in accordance with the micro-topology. The flow of the river water is slow, as if teaching us about the precious passage of time.

All of these moderate and sensitive components form a scene which depicts the essence of what Uemura felt and how he lived. The scene is also a fundamental impression of nature which is felt deeply by most Japanese people.

When Uemura embarked on a trip, his aim was not to attempt to conquer the awesome forces of nature but rather to make himself part of it and to follow in suit of what nature had to offer. The concept for the museum evolved from the planners' appreciation of Uemura's respect for a meaningful dialogue with the natural environment.

The design of the complex builds on this essential relationship while seeking to contribute to the improvement of the natural environment of Uemura's birth-place. The planners wished to realise an 'environmental totality' by integrating nature, architecture and an exhibition to represent the spirit of the adventurer.

A continuous path is symbolic of the explorer's 'Challenge to Distance'; at the same time it conveys the image of a crevice that cuts the ground surface sharply.

Starting with an inclined approach, the exhibition rooms, library and screen-projection room are strung out along the continuous path. This runs through the building towards the terrace which extends over the pond. A glass skylight, which is evocative of an ice ridge, projects above ground. This provides natural light for the underground passage and serves as a 'memorial wall' with descriptions of Uemura's life and achievements.

Visitors to the museum gain a sense of the incredible achievements of Uemura and leave the building with an impression of his life and his special relationship with nature. At night, the 'memorial wall' is distinguished as a streak of light in the darkness, symbolising the strength of will in the face of unpredictable nature.

KIYOSATO MUSEUM OF PHOTOGRAPHIC ART
Kiyosato, Japan

Kiyosato, in Yamanasi Prefecture, is well-known as a health resort and is increasingly the location of new guest houses and souvenir shops. Museums and concert halls have also been constructed recently, establishing a new image of Kiyosato as a place to enjoy not only nature but also art. The Kiyosato Museum of Photographic Art, which was completed in 1995, is one of the newly-constructed facilities.

The complex combines a photographic art museum and a lodging facility. It is surrounded by a natural environment with rich greenery and magnificent views of Mount Fuji in the south and Mount Yatsugatake in the north.

By the time Akira Kuryu & Associates took part in the development plan for the Kiyosato Museum of Photographic Art, all the trees had been cleared from the site

and the primary land preparation had been completed. A geometrical structure was designed that would cover the prepared site, with the inner spaces of the building and the artificial outer spaces conceived in such a way as to promote complete harmony with the 18 gardens that are scattered around the building.

The inner spaces were expected to be integrated as much as possible with the surrounding environment. The furniture inside is designed to be part of the main structure. Accordingly, some pieces of furniture on the first floor are connected with those on the second floor and other pieces protrude from the exterior wall of the building.

Thus, not only are the displayed works in the exhibition rooms presented to

visitors for consideration but also the landscape, furniture, and structure of the building.

The combination of a museum and a lodging facility was not planned solely for the convenience of visitors. The concept behind this is the creation of an utterly new space through merging two different facilities, providing visitors with the experience of staying overnight in a museum or establishing an accommodation facility equipped with museum facilities. The central passage which runs through all these facilities forms a well-hole with a skylight and effectively connects the intertwined functions.

The interaction between landscape, furniture, and building responds to the architects' desire to create an environmental totality.

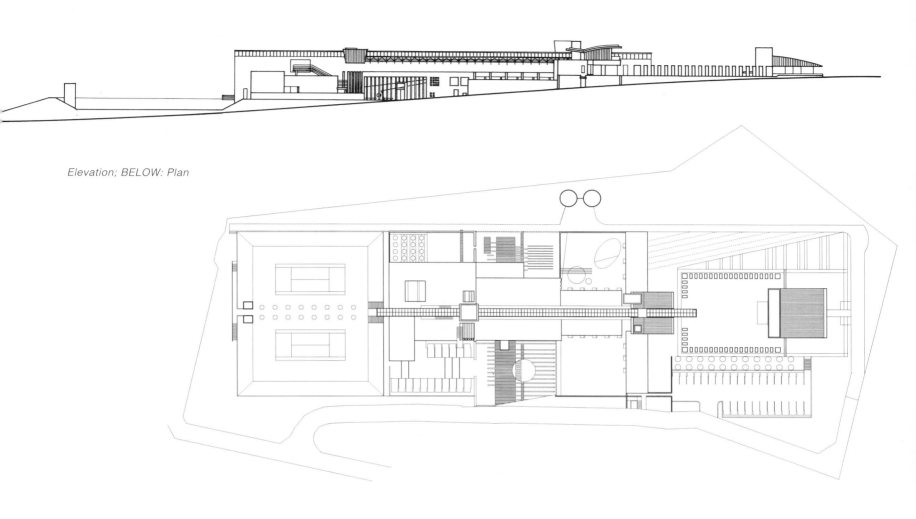

Elevation; BELOW: Plan

85

TONAMI TULIP GALLERY
Tonami, Japan

Tonami City, in Toyama Prefecture, is known as the leading centre for tulip production in Japan. The Tonami Tulip Fair, held for two weeks before and after the tulip-flowering season, attracts more than 400,000 visitors. The Tonami Tulip Gallery (1994-96) was designed to be the main attraction of the fair and a place for people to enjoy tulips all through the year.

The tulip originated in Turkey and was imported to Japan via Holland in recent times. The varieties of the plant had been improved in these countries before reaching Japan and taking root in the snowy province of Tonami, far from the tulip's country of origin.

The plan of the gallery is based on the concept of the building as a representation of the union of two different natural features. Two images were planned to be blended harmoniously into a single facility – one is the image of an Islamic culture which flourished on the firm ground of Central Asia; the other is the image of a village relating to the unique style of community on the Tonami Plain (houses scattered in the paddy fields, each maintaining a cedar grove).

The latter image is embodied in the design of the atrium floating in the water basin, while the relationship between the house and surrounding grove (used for protection against the wind) is reflected in the arrangement of the Islamic space which is enclosed by the atrium.

The articulation of the dome, a number of columns, and umbrella-shaped tents expresses the geometrical composition of Islamic space. A natural atmosphere is created that is closely associated with the climate of Central Asia.

The facilities of the gallery complex (resource exhibition room, plant and flower display rooms, a cafeteria, shops, and clerical work spaces etc) are distributed in a way that evokes the bazaars, paths and plazas found in Islamic towns and cities.

Section; BELOW: Plan

OKAZAKI ART AND HISTORICAL MUSEUM: MINDSCAPE MUSEUM
Okazaki, Japan

The Okazaki Art and Historical Museum was planned to be the central facility in the cultural zone developed in the Okazaki City Centre General Park (Okazaki-Shi Chuo Sogo Koen Park) and was completed in 1996. The site, which inclines to the edge of a pond, is surrounded by a lush natural environment with rich greenery. The museum thus provides the citizens with a place for recreation and relaxation.

In planning the project for this particular location, one of the important problems to be solved concerning preservation of the area was that of handling the large volume of the building, which was to be equipped with such spaces as repository and exhibition halls. Following careful and detailed examination, it was decided to integrate the museum building with the topography by embedding the inner spaces under the inclined ground surface.

Visible above the ground surface are an atrium (which also serves as the entrance hall to the museum) and a restaurant with light-weight roofing. The restaurant offers pleasant views of the surface of the pond and surrounding greenery on the hill as well as providing an unobstructed view of Okazaki city.

This museum is the first of its kind in Japan to focus on the 'mind' as its theme. Exhibitions relating to this particular theme will be held on a consistent basis and the number of works of art or exhibits in the collection is to be increased gradually.

Most of the operation policies of public art museums and historical museums have placed priority on the hardware aspects of such an undertaking. However, with the Okazaki Art and Historical Museum, software aspects are to be given priority to allow the museum to grow organically. The museum is perceived as one which will 'grow with time', as a 'developing body'.

The exhibition at the Okazaki Art and Historical Museum is not confined to the facilities inside the building. On the contrary, the museum also presents objects for exhibition in the natural environment that surrounds it. A total design of the site and the landscape was advocated in order to realise a 'museum in the form of a park', or a 'park in the form of a museum'.

The arrangement of a water wall – using the museum signboard – a water basin and a cascade forms a 'water axis' towards the pond. Similarly, a 'wind axis' is created along the main approach path to the museum by eight windmills, a slope covered with low, striped bamboo trees (whose leaves rustle when they wave in the wind) and lines of tulip trees (liriodendrons).

A sculpture by Fujiko Nakaya is placed at the intersection of the two axes. This symbolises natural light, wind and water, and heightens the visitors' awareness of the environment. The sculpture is also designed to portray fog as it would appear in a natural setting. The windmills with their arms turning in the wind, the leaves and treetops swaying with the breeze, the ever-changing fog, and the flowing or falling water are 'moving' attractions, accommodated in an 'inactive' background formed by the surrounding greenery. They effectively provide the visitor with a natural progression into the world of art.

In Japan, museums have long been looked upon as places for contemplation or as facilities for enlightenment. In addition to providing this service, the Okazaki Art and Historical Museum is equipped with a museum shop and restaurant. Moreover, a harmonious and relaxing environment is created by the relationship between the museum facilities and the greenery-rich environment.

Thus, the overall atmosphere of this museum introduces a new type of museum that is integrated with the environment. The museum is redefined as a place for enjoyment and as a 'museum garden' that is open to all.

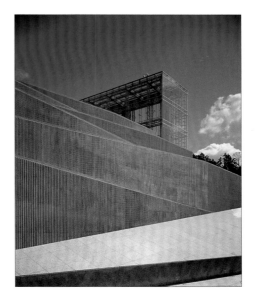

DEREK WALKER ASSOCIATES
ROYAL ARMOURIES MUSEUM
Leeds, UK

In June 1991 the Trustees of the Royal Armouries at the Tower of London announced that the greater part of its unique collection of arms and armour would move from the Tower to a new building at Clarence Dock in Leeds.

Open to the public at the Tower for more than 300 years, The Royal Armouries is Britain's oldest museum, and with some 40,000 exhibits, one of the world's leading collections of arms, armour and weapons. The 37-acre site for the new museum is less than a mile from the M1/M62 motorways to the south, and a few minutes from central Leeds to the north.

In 1992 Derek Walker Associates won the competition for the master plan sponsored by the Development Corporation and was subsequently asked by the trustees to design the building itself and all the interior galleries, displays and supporting facilities.

The DWA master plan sites the museum on a promontory between the historic Clarence Dock built in 1843 and the River Aire. The plan includes a tiltyard for demonstrations of tournaments and hunting techniques, a menagerie court for the care and display of animals and birds used in performances, and a craft court to demonstrate the making and conservation of armour and weapons.

To complement and support the museum, the outer dock is transformed into a busy, active and colourful space with performance areas, shops, including a chandlery, cafés, bars and restaurants, eating-out areas, sheltered arcades for window shopping and market stalls. There are moorings for visiting leisure craft, an historic craft exhibit and a jetty for the river bus service to central Leeds.

The building itself is designed to be informal, comprehensible and dramatic. Entry is from the dockside and from the main parking area to the south via an internal public street rising 30 metres through the building.

The Street is the focus of all the museum's circulation routes including the Hall of Steel, a lofty, internally lit octagonal stair tower which contains a massive display of 3,200 pieces of arms and armour and forms the main link between the museum's six gallery levels. At ground level the Street and temporary exhibition gallery can be used for banquets, concerts, meetings and other community events.

The collection is divided into five major galleries, the War Gallery, the Tournament Gallery, the Oriental Gallery, and the Self Defence and Hunting Galleries. The pieces to be displayed range from the sumptuously ornamented armour and weaponry of kings and courtiers of past centuries, to the plain, functional, sometimes throwaway weapons of the modern soldier.

The museum, which was opened in 1996, intends to entertain, instruct and inspire its many visitors. In addition to the five main galleries there is a 300-seat auditorium, a temporary exhibition gallery, a children's interactive gallery and a newsroom where current world events are discussed in relation to the main gallery themes. There is also a large restaurant, bar and bistro and refreshment areas on each floor of the building.

Model

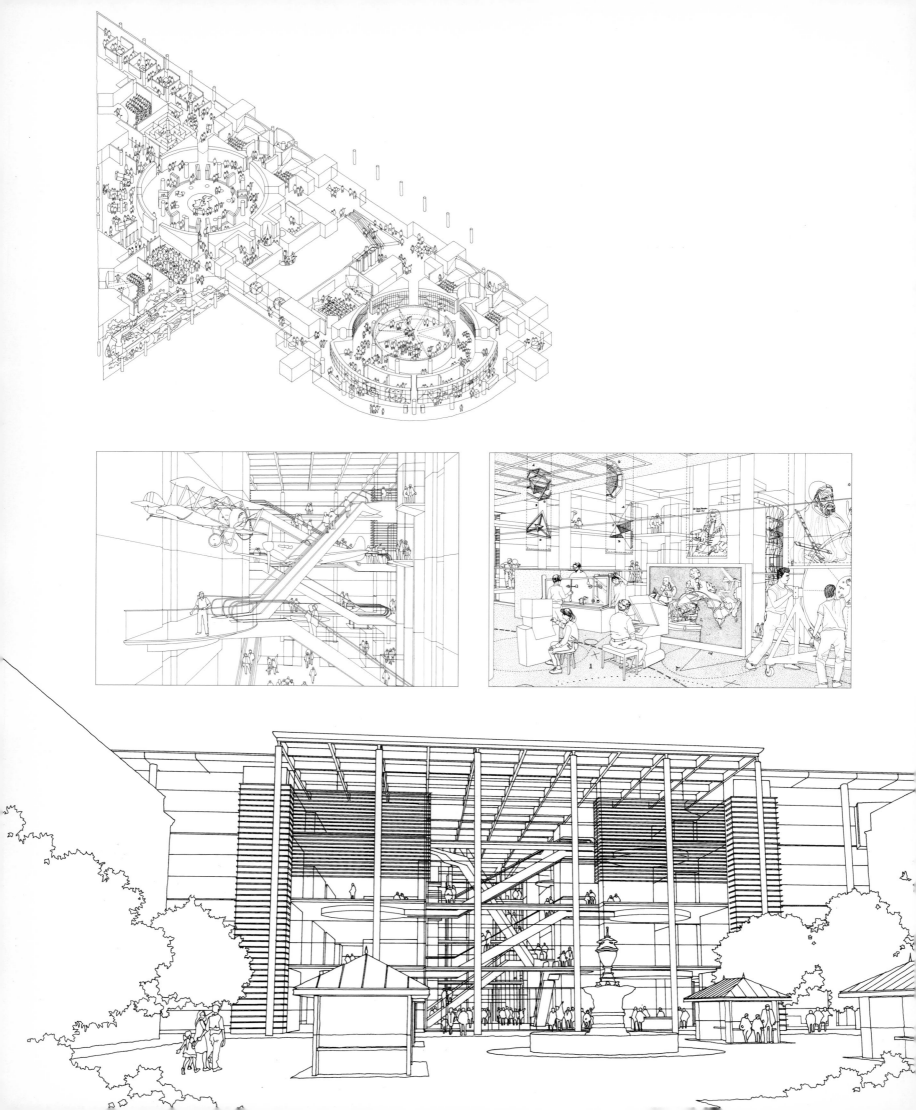

MUSEUM OF BRITISH HISTORY
London

Derek Walker Associates has developed a building strategy for the Museum of British History at St Bartholomew's which recognises the need to design and construct a major new building in proximity to the listed 18th-century hospital blocks, while creating a visually exciting presentation aimed at maximising visitor use of the site.

This is achieved by integrating the new building as the southern facade to the central square formed by the existing buildings and by their restorative refurbishment as support accommodation.

The strategy envisaged three levels of galleries in adjacent buildings which are interlinked dynamically by a glazed atrium running their full height within which are placed dynamic displays. The galleries sit above a freely accessed ground floor enclosed piazza, off which are the museum shop, restaurants, temporary exhibition area and ticketing. The basement level allows secure and discrete servicing.

The Museum of British History will fill a significant gap in the museum sector, presenting a showcase of the history of Britain and its people from earliest times through to the present day. Whilst other museums provide excellent showcases of specific aspects of Britain's history, none gives the comprehensive picture that will be provided by the Museum of British History. This will be a new national museum to complement and reinforce the appeal of our existing national and regional museums.

The choice of location within London is vital to the museum's future success and considerable research has gone into finding the right site. Many sites have been considered but St Bartholomew's has been selected for a number of key

reasons including: excellent public transport links, the ability to provide space for the new 300,000 square feet (28,000 square metre) museum building with the opportunity for further development in adjacent existing buildings, and close proximity to a number of established visitor attractions.

Perhaps the greatest challenge in developing the museum has been distilling more than 2,000 years of history into 161,000 square feet (15,000 square metres) of display space. Two steps have been taken to enable this to happen. The first has been the careful selection of five core themes that will form the subject matter for the main galleries. They are:
– *The British People*: an explanation of the invasions, events, immigration and other factors that have resulted in the richly diverse and polyglot nation that Britain is today.
– *Politics and The Monarchy*: clearly no history of Britain would be complete without politics and the monarchy, highlighting the key personalities and milestone events. This particular theme also helps to provide something of a familiar sense of chronology to British history.
– *Language and Culture*: a celebration of our language and how it has changed with time. A focus not only on great British authors, playwrights and dramatists who have used the language to such great effect but on art, music, the performing arts and on the development of popular culture and entertainment.
– *The British Landscape*: a vivid demonstration of how the physical state of Britain has evolved and the impact of man's endeavours to influence and enhance that process by adapting, cultivating and exploiting the land.
– *Invention, Science and Technology*:

focusing on the wealth of Britain's creative genius and innovation over the centuries and demonstrating how science and technology have transformed our lifestyles.

The second step has been the adoption of a building design strategy to deliver a purpose-designed building that accommodates, in addition to all the necessary support and back-up services, a comprehensive range of presentational techniques, including traditional galleries and displays, live performance areas, cinemas, video walls and interactive zones. By mixing presentational formats in this way, a wider range of subjects can be covered and visitors will be better able to absorb and retain information. This approach not only suits the design needs of the museum but will create a truly compelling attraction.

Each of the five core themes is worthy of a museum in its own right. When viewed together they represent a substantial mass which will require and deserve a number of hours for visitors to experience fully. Nevertheless, it is accepted that there is a clear need to provide for time-constrained visitors to experience the museum and gain a reasonably structured and comprehensive, albeit brief, overview of British history.

Therefore, there needs to be a way in which those visitors with only one to one-and-a-half hours to spare can still obtain a worthwhile experience from a visit to the museum. This will be achieved through the provision of an overview gallery, providing a summary of the museum's scope. Rather than make the overview gallery a separate entity it is conceived as the 'hub' of the composition with five 'spokes': the main themes. In summary, therefore, the Museum of British History will have six galleries.

OPPOSITE, FROM ABOVE L TO R: Axonometric of third floor; perspective view of the atrium; internal perspective of the Exploratorium; external perspective, view from the square

EXPERIENCE OR INTERPRETATION
THE DILEMMA OF MUSEUMS OF MODERN ART
Nicholas Serota

The following extract is the concluding part of a lecture given by Nicholas Serota, Director of the Tate Gallery, London, for The Walter Neurath Memorial Lectures, on 13 March 1996 at the National Gallery in London. The lecture was published by Thames and Hudson in 1996. This extract is preceded by an account of changes in the nature of art, in the ambition of the artist and in methods of display – for example, from the historical interpretive hang to the single-artist presentation that became prevalent in the 1980s – and the effect of these changes on the conventions of the museum.

What do we expect from museums of modern art at the end of the twentieth century? We may agree that the encyclopaedic and dictionary functions of the museum are neither achievable nor desirable. But there is less general agreement on how to balance the interests of the artist, the curator and the visitor. Some of the larger institutions have begun to explore new approaches. However, the most stimulating developments have occurred in smaller museums, where the sense of institutional responsibility towards conventional expectations is less pressing.

One influential model is the Hallen für Neue Kunst in Schaffhausen, Switzerland. The institution occupies three floors of a former textile factory which is lit by windows on both sides. The open floors are divided into a sequence of spaces rather than chambers. Artists are generally represented by several works presented as clusters, which has the effect of creating overlapping and merging zones of influence. As a result, unexpected readings and comparisons occur.

Schaffhausen draws together artists of approximately the same generation and of related sensibilities. Greater daring is present at the Insel Hombroich, an isolated private museum established by Karl Heinz Müller on a wasteland at Neuss outside Düsseldorf.[1] Müller houses his collection in a series of pavilions constructed to the designs of the sculptor Erwin Heerich. These are strikingly simple but offer considerable variety, with rectangular and square rooms, and even some asymmetrical, of different heights and proportions arranged in contrasting plans. Each has its singular quality of light and volume. Müller adds to this complexity by showing work from earlier cultures alongside contemporary art and by making surprising comparisons, as in the display devoted to Fautrier and Corinth, both represented by exemplary groups of works.

Such juxtapositions are perhaps a more natural strategy for the private collector, or for the exhibition maker, than for the museum curator. In recent years, exhibitions and displays have been presented according to this dialectical principle with increasing frequency. The main room in the exhibition *A New Spirit in Painting* at the Royal Academy in 1981 brought together three artists of two generations, Balthus, de Kooning and Baselitz, in an assembly which disclosed unexpected parallels and contrasts between three contemporary approaches to the figure.

A comparable strategy, devised by Rudi Fuchs for *documenta 7* in Kassel in 1982, was subsequently introduced to the museum at Castello di Rivoli outside Turin in 1984, and more recently in a series of so-called 'Couplet' exhibitions at the Stedelijk Museum in Amsterdam.[2] According to the Fuchs principle, works by a single artist are dispersed to different parts of the exhibition or museum. On each encounter another aspect of the work is emphasised. At best this broadens and complicates the spectator's understanding of the work, though for some viewers these juxtapositions can sometimes appear perverse or obscure.[3]

I have been suggesting that a willingness to engage in personal interpretation, to risk offence by unexpected confrontation, can yield rewards. Nowhere is this curatorial courage more evident than at the new Museum für Moderne Kunst in Frankfurt. From unpromising beginnings, Jean-Christophe Ammann has created a dynamic and often challenging view of the art of the 1960s and 1990s.

The building, by Hans Hollein, occupies a wedge-shaped plot and was completed in 1991. Hollein resolved some of the awkward geometries of the site by grouping his galleries on three floors around the high central room. But it remains a difficult building in which to install art. Ammann has responded with wit, inviting artists to occupy spaces designated as service spaces. Ammann works, as he says, 'from the perspective of my mind's eye'[4] and has sought to bring appropriate works into rooms with a particular character, as in a triangular room containing a sculpture by Katharina Fritsch. But he has not shied away from interpretation, grouping works and artists which seem to connect with one another in what he terms 'climatic zones', a process comparable with the zones of influence which I have identified at Schaffhausen. Ammann does not arrange temporary loan exhibitions. Certain installations and rooms in the museum are permanent. Others change on a periodic basis as works are added to the collection, creating new confrontations and echoes.

One final example may serve as a cautionary reminder that stasis also remains a valuable component of the museum. Permanent installation offers an encounter with a particular work of art within a given space where change is brought about not by new juxtapositions but by the changing natural light at different times of the day and by the changing perspective of the viewer. This was the ideal that drove Donald Judd to create a new form of museum at Marfa, Texas in the late 1970s.[5] Judd was critical of the way in which museums display contemporary art in anthologies of short duration. At Marfa he took a range of disused military buildings and with removals of sparing economy and finely judged additions designed by himself, he created space in which to show his work extensively and that of others in selected installations. As installations they are exemplary; as an experience of the work they afford a deep and measured view. And from this example lessons have been learned with regard for the need in museums for places of prolonged concentration and contemplation.

However, we have seen how 'experience' can become a formula. The best museums of the future will, like Schaffhausen, Insel Hombroich and Frankfurt, seek to promote different modes and levels of 'interpretation' by subtle juxtapositions of 'experience'. Some rooms and works will be fixed, the pole star around which others will turn. In this way we can expect to create a matrix of changing relationships to be explored by visitors according to their particular interests and sensibilities. In the new museum, each of us, curators and visitors alike, will have to become more willing to chart our own path, redrawing the map of modern art, rather than following a single path laid down by a curator.

We have come a long way from Sir Charles Eastlake's chrono-logical hang by school [Eastlake became Director of the National Gallery, London in 1855], but the educational and aesthetic purpose is no less significant. One-artist displays have a part to play, especially in presenting site-specific work and in facilitating concentration, but in my view we still need a curator to stimulate readings of the collection and to establish those 'climatic zones' which can enrich our appreciation and understanding of the art of this century. Our aim must be to generate a condition in which visitors can experience a sense of discovery in looking at particular paintings, sculptures or installations in a particular room at a particular moment, rather than find themselves standing on the conveyor belt of history.

Notes

1 See Paul Good, *Hermes or the Philosphy of the Island of Hombroich*, Neuss, 1987.
2 See especially Rudi Fuchs, *documenta 7*, Kassel, 1983, and *Ouverture*, Castello di Rivoli, Turin, 1984.
3 See Philip Peters, 'Back to the Front Line! The Stedelijk Museum after five "Couplets"', *Kunst & Museumjournaal*, vol 6, no 3/4, 1995, pp49-54.
4 Jean-Christophe Ammann, *From the Perspective of my Mind's Eye*, Museum für Moderne Kunst, Frankfurt, 1991.
5 See Donald Judd, *Raüme/Spaces*, Wiesbaden Museum, 1993.

Hans Hollein, Museum für Moderne Kunst, Frankfurt-am-Main, view of the central room

museum (mju:ˈzɪəm) *n.* a place or building where objects of historical, artistic, or scientific interest are exhibited, preserved or studied. [C17: via Latin from Greek *Mouseion* home of the Muses, from *Mousa* MUSE]

Collins English Dictionary

Marcel Duchamp was once asked what for him was the difference between sculpture and architecture. He thought for a moment . . . and then said, 'plumbing'! . . . We have various tasks that are implied by the word museum: preservation, conservation and the availability of almost a library of works, which certainly calls for certain things. Most of the contemporary work I am interested in deals with context. And of course when you are invited to work in a museum, you are dealing very much with an institutional context . . . The approach to the work is organised very much by the history of that institution and what has preceded your own work. Often the architecture reflects the institutional texture and so you actually come down to struggling with rather pragmatic things. Maybe I am just reflecting my own position, but I have found that architecture in relation to art should be neutralised in a way that serves art. The meaning of the architecture should be useable.

Joseph Kosuth

Museums should be built to serve art and not architecture. The design of new museums should be based on an understanding of the nature and requirements of modern and contemporary art. These thoughts should be too obvious to need to be stated. The depressing evidence of most of the museums built over the past 20 or 30 years, however, necessitates their restatement.

Michael Craig Martin

The notion that museums are in stasis is fundamentally in conflict with the historical record and the Museum of Installation (MOI) presents an option in the continuous evolution of the presentation and preservation of the artwork. We are careful to note that we do not save the art object, as this is for other museums to do. MOI preserves merely the documentation of the past existence of the time-based work, and in a way the idea of the work. Our archive is a repository for thoughts as well as for deeds. The actions of the artists in our sites are documented by photographs, videos, slides, catalogues and artists' proposals in much the same way as conventional museums, but this documentation is for us all important as the work ceases to exist on its dismantling. To preserve the artefacts, the mere objects of the installations, would be a betrayal of our ideals. So the museum exists as a platform for the creation of art, and the preservation of the idea of that art – a temporary house for contemporary muses.

Michael Petry

But museums do, in spite of everything, continually evolve, and if they have no more permanent references, the works will be weakened. There is no architectural remedy for this; the museum cannot pastiche its former self as a cultural structure. Those works which require a respectful, refined, neutral space will be best served by a simplified, well-proportioned gallery of a traditional sort. Those that are contrived by artists to envelop the perceptual organs of the viewer can usually be constructed for limited periods in any large, unobstructed space and may be as much at home in a 19th-century gallery as in a warehouse, since the underlying architecture can be hidden as necessary, provided appropriate services can be laid on. Those that come alive only when located in the 'real' world should not be accommodated by specially designed galleries until they have become corpses. Exhibiting them in old churches, warehouses and factories gives them charm, but only attenuated vitality.

Michael Compton

I believe it is important for a museum or a gallery to have a fixed location because people are used to coming to a place to see art. If you have a moving gallery like the Museum of Installation, it will only appeal to the converted who are willing to seek it out. I don't think you can expect architecture to constantly change in order to keep up with other forms of art. Artists' materials and manifestations continuously change: the constant factor, in my opinion, is that galleries contain audiences who go there to look at things. An important issue to be addressed is the identity of the audience for contemporary art. I think that too often it is assumed that people are willing to look at contemporary art and to understand it. I would like to see the gallery become a place where people feel that they can debate, discuss and create meanings for themselves.

Anna Harding

We, that is, Coop Himmelblau, believe that a good museum of the future will, in the next century, make art obsolete. We have never liked museums. We used to prefer going to rock concerts. But now that rock concerts have become increasingly louder and our hearing has become poorer, we usually escape to the silent, quiet, obliging museum. Thus I have arrived at the assumption that museums are for more mature people.

Wolf Prix

The museum is that which enables distortion of time, place and frequency for the enjoyment and edification of the voluntary user. The enclosure or shell is a protection, a signpost, an advertisement and an 'icon'.

Dr Alan Borg

I see museums, in a sense, as the churches of today, without thinking of an institutionalised spirituality. A museum is a place in which, when confronted by an object, one can experience some kind of inner depth in a very individual and free way. So the place where this will happen, especially in the 21st century, is going to be very important. The museum is not only about spirituality, it is also about politics. So many aspects of life have their place in the museum. We have seen the museum develop from being a place where we see material objects, paintings or sculptures. In the future, I can see it growing into a completely different institution: the sort of place where people can come in and pick up new ideas in many different ways.

Louwrien Wijers

Everything today is becoming staged . . . It is not only Disney that recreates the past for us in an easy and simple way, it is now serious museums that make entertainment for us so that their museum becomes an attraction on the tourist route. It seems to me that we are now competing for the attention of a public where the standards are provided by department stores, shopping malls and airports, and no longer by churches.

Robert Maxwell